**Other books by Robert U. Akeret**

*Not by Words Alone*

*Photoanalysis*

*Family Tales / Family Wisdom*
(with Daniel Klein)

# Tales from a
# Traveling Couch

# Tales from a Traveling Couch

*A Psychotherapist Revisits His*

*Most Memorable Patients*

## ROBERT U. AKERET

W · W · NORTON & COMPANY · NEW YORK · LONDON

Printed in the United States of America.

FIRST EDITION

*The text of this book is composed in Aster with the display type set in Windsor.*
*Composition and manufacturing by the Maple-Vail Book Manufacturing Group.*
*Book design by Marjorie J. Flock.*

Some names, events, places, and identifying details have been altered to as-
sure the privacy of all concerned.

Library of Congress Cataloging-in-Publication Data

Akeret, Robert U., 1928–
     Tales from a traveling couch / Robert U. Akeret.
          p.     cm.
     1. Psychotherapy patients—Case Studies.   2. Psychotherapy
patients—Longitudinal studies.   3. Psychotherapy—Evaluation——Case
studies.   I. Title.
RC465.A34     1995
616.89'14—dc20                                              94-36068

ISBN 0-393-03779-7

W. W. Norton & Company, Inc., 500 Fifth Avenue, New York, N.Y. 10110
W. W. Norton & Company Ltd., 10 Coptic Street, London WC1A 1PU

          1 2 3 4 5 6 7 8 9 0

To my patients,
my teachers

R. U. A.

# Contents

Prologue: The Traveling Couch . . . . . . . . . *15*

1. Naomi: The Dancer from the Dance . . . . . . *19*

2. Charles: The Soul of Love . . . . . . . . . *58*

3. Seth: The Real Thing . . . . . . . . . . . *101*

4. Mary: Beware What You Desire . . . . . . . *144*

5. Sasha: The Beast . . . . . . . . . . . . *181*

Epilogue: Final Analysis . . . . . . . . . . *225*

Acknowledgments . . . . . . . . . . *239*

"To me, psychoanalysis is a vital art that demands more of its practitioners than the clever exercise of their brains. Into its practice also goes the heart, and there are occasions when human feelings take precedence over the rituals and dogmas of the craft."

Robert Lindner
*The Fifty-Minute Hour*

"To restore the human subject at the centre—the suffering, afflicted, fighting human subject—we must deepen a case history to a narrative or tale; only then do we have a 'who' as well as a 'what', a real person."

Oliver Sacks
*The Man Who Mistook His Wife for a Hat*

# Tales from a Traveling Couch

# Prologue: The Traveling Couch

I am not inviting you to follow me, but to follow yourself.

Georg Groddeck, *The Book of the It*

THERE IS ONE awful frustration built into being a psychotherapist: I never know how the story ends.

When a patient walks out of my office after our final session, that is it. The rest of his or her life remains a mystery to me.

To engage someone in therapy is ultimately to offer her an alternative life. She may seek my help because she is in psychological pain or because her marriage is in ruins or because she is bedeviled by voices in her head, but in some fundamental sense it is always a new life that she is after—a better, more satisfying life. From the start I try to imagine what that alternative life could be and how I can help her script it. But just at the moment she seems strong enough to get on with this new life on her own—when that script is finally ready to be enacted—I am banned from the theater.

How did it play out?

Could she sustain her adopted identity as a Spanish contessa? Did his psychosexual obsession with a circus bear ever possess him again? Was he able to resist his mother's relentless sabotage of his marriage? Did he ever write another novel? Did she ever "murder" again?

And above all else, was life sweet? Was it full?

Sweeter and fuller than it would have been if he or she had never entered my office in the first place?

My world is lopsided with prologues, bereft of endings. It is as if someone had ripped the last pages from all the novels in my library. Not simply my curiosity is frustrated, but my aesthetic.

Yet my frustration runs far deeper than that. After devoting my entire adult life to helping people examine and change their lives, I don't really know if I have been effective. How can I possibly, if I don't know what becomes of my patients after their therapy comes to an end? In the final analysis I don't know if my life's work has been successful because there is no final analysis.

Sometimes it seems preposterous to me to believe that therapy works at all. Typically, when a patient enters my office the first time, his personality and all its attendant problems are the result of hundreds of thousands of hours of living. How can the two of us hope to effect genuine change in only a few hundred isolated hours, often less? I am speaking of change that reaches into the very core of his being—fundamental change in the way he experiences his life, not simply "reformed" behavior.

But it does happen. I have seen therapy work. I have seen people pierce their delusions, throw off their obsessions, conquer their phobias. Again and again I have seen a person release himself from a desperately unhappy life and learn the language of an alternative one. Over the past thirty-five years I have seen this particular miracle happen hundreds of times.

But does it last? Do the changes hold? Or when my back is turned, does it all unravel? Does the power of those hundreds of thousands of hours that preceded therapy reassert itself and take back all that we have fought for?

Certainly there are a great number of follow-up studies on the effectiveness of various psychotherapies. Most are based on responses to questionnaires sent out to patients a year after termination of treatment. One study—a favorite of mine— compares a group that had been in client-centered therapy with a control group that had been given dogs as companions. (They found no difference.) But of course, none of these studies tells me anything about my patients. And further, where individual lives are concerned, there can be no control group. The only meaningful controls exist in our minds and in our imaginations:

Is this the life I hoped for?

Is this the life I hoped to avoid?

I am an obsessive therapist; I cannot stop thinking about my patients. I find myself ineluctably drawn to patients who have had great upheavals and pain in their childhoods, as I had in my own. If I have any special aptitude for my work, it is this: Nothing human is alien to me. There is hardly an obsession or delusion, terror or doubt that I cannot imagine having myself.

So in the end my deepest frustration grows out of something far more personal and painful than simply the absence of scientific data to validate my casework. I have found that in order to be successful, the therapeutic process must reach a degree of intimacy that the brittle, technical words *transference* and *countertransference* cannot begin to describe. The truth is that a devoted loving bond usually develops between myself and my patients, and when a patient walks out of my office for the last time, it is as if a child I have nurtured to maturity were leaving home. I am at once exhilarated and despondent. This is the moment we have been working toward all along, yet it is a moment I have come to dread; I may never hear from her again. It can be heartbreaking.

I recently turned sixty-six years old, an age when many of my contemporaries find themselves rummaging through old yearbooks and yellowed correspondence, making blind phone calls late at night to long-lost friends and lovers as they search for strands of their pasts, tracking down what was and what might have been—their alternative lives.

As for me, I find myself in the thrall of a single question: Whatever happened to my former patients?

Last year I started tracking some of them down, making blind phone calls late at night all around America and Europe. Although the general rule of psychotherapy is that the therapist should never intrude uninvited into a patient's life, I decided that enough time had passed to render this rule moot. Further, I promised myself that if any of the voices on the other end of the line sounded remotely hesitant, I would not pursue any further. But none did.

Then, one sunny morning last April, possessed by equal parts of curiosity and anxiety, I got into my Plymouth Voyager and set off on a remarkable journey—a journey in search of story endings.

# Naomi: The Dancer from the Dance

O chestnut tree, great rooted blossomer,
Are you the leaf, the blossom or the bole?
O body swayed to music, O brightening glance,
How can we know the dancer from the dance?

—William Butler Yeats, "Among School Children"

**M**IDWAY THROUGH the Lincoln Tunnel I slipped *Sketches of Spain* into the tape deck and turned the volume way up. The castanets crackled around me like cicadas on a summer night, and then those mournful horns wailed in, pleading, soaring, filling the van. The piece has been one of my favorites since I first heard it in the early sixties— Miles Davis at his sinuous, soulful best. It is his and Gil Evans's riff on Joaquín Rodrigo's *Concierto de Aranjuez,* which was itself inspired by Spanish folk melodies. There are purists who put down *Sketches* as synthetic and false, a dilution of the authentic folk idiom. Not me; for my money, Davis honed to the essence of that idiom and blew it true. But God knows I have never been accused of being a purist, not even thirty-five years ago, when I was just out of graduate school, freshly imbued with that most orthodox of doctrines, Freudian psychology.

An arch of brilliant sunlight appeared straight ahead of me, and I accelerated out of the tunnel, smiling as I circled up the ramp, Manhattan shimmering across the Hudson on my right. I was on my way to Miami, the home of Isabella Cortez, née

Naomi Goldberg, one of my first patients at my first job, therapist with the counseling staff of the City College of New York.

I'd thought about Naomi hundreds of times over the past three and half decades. She'd stuck in my mind like a first important teacher—or a first lover. From the start Naomi tested me, tested not merely my newly acquired psychological knowledge and technique but my flexibility of mind and independence of spirit—my mettle. Naomi was a test I was always afraid I'd failed.

She was the first destination on my itinerary.

The directions were simple: interconnecting parkways and turnpikes all the way down the Atlantic coast. I'd never even considered taking an airplane. Everything I needed was inside this van: tape deck, memo recorder, notebooks, a carton full of case records, my guitar. My traveling cocoon. I looked up at myself in the rearview mirror, saw a grinning bald head. My God, I hadn't taken a trip like this since I was a young man without wife or children—or grandchildren, for that matter. I felt giddy and more than a little apprehensive. I turned the Miles Davis tape up even louder. It was the last cut, a flamenco song called "Solea," Andalusian for "loneliness."

"Miss Goldberg is disruptive and provocative both in the classroom and in student activities. Her behavior and dress are grossly inappropriate. Please see her immediately."

Naomi's referral had come to me in a manila envelope from Dean Yates of the college's Office of Student Life. Written in pen at the bottom of the page was a note from my boss, Dr. Briscoe, supervisor of student counseling:

Robert,
Take a full hour with this one. You may experience some difficulty.
                                                            D. B.
P.S. Miss G. has been told she's being seen for vocational counseling.

I'd like to report that I felt a flash of resentment at the deliberate deception of my prospective client that was admitted in that "P.S.," but that would not be accurate. My primary reaction was curiosity. The counseling service was so under-staffed at the time that almost all sessions were limited to twenty-five minutes, even in some cases of students with chronic depression or excessive drinking problems. Why in the world did Miss Naomi Goldberg merit a full hour? Just how disruptive could she be?

There is something I must not forget: the year. It was 1957. Dwight D. Eisenhower was president. Gloria Steinem was in high school—a cheerleader, I believe. Most college girls wore circle pins on white blouses with Peter Pan collars; if they were particularly gifted students, they were encouraged to become teachers or social workers. *Nymphomaniac* was the technical term for women who were as avid about sex as men. I was thirty; I had just begun to lose my hair.

I tried to locate a free private office or unoccupied class-room for my first appointed hour with Miss Goldberg, but none was available, so I had to settle for my personal quarters, a thin-walled six-by-six cubicle in the midst of a maze of iden-tical cubicles occupied by mathematics professors. Through these walls I would often hear sudden and enthusiastic rapid-fire bursts about $X$'s and $Y$'s, polygons and googoleplexes. It was as though a devotee of Kafka had been commissioned to design a space for the most intimate human exchanges.

At precisely 10:00 A.M. the buzzer in my cubicle sounded. Before I could rise, Naomi Goldberg walked through the door.

To say that she was an attractive young woman would not begin to capture the effect that Naomi created as she swung into my tiny office. She was stunning, a voluptuous, long-legged beauty with raven hair and fiery dark eyes that locked on mine immediately. She was wearing neither a circle pin nor a Peter Pan blouse, but rather a crimson wool sweater over a skintight body-length black leotard. She raised her shoulders in a gesture somewhere between a shimmy and a shrug and smiled.

"Mmm, it's warm in here, Doctor," she said in a throaty voice. "Mind if I slip this off?"

Without waiting for a reply, she crossed her arms in front of her, grasped the lip of her sweater, and slowly pulled it up, undulating first her hips and then her torso as she wriggled free of the garment. Clearly she was not wearing a bra under her leotard. With a flourish she dropped the sweater onto the floor. Her eyes had never left mine. She shook her long hair behind her and smiled again, triumphantly. Defiantly.

Yes, "disruptive in the classroom" seemed within the realm of possibility.

And yet, although dazzled by Naomi's entrance, I did not feel in the least aroused by her. To be sure, I was well prepared: I had been repeatedly warned by my mentors about seductive patients; I had been trained not to give away any sexual feelings I felt for them. But the truth was I hadn't experienced any sexual feelings that I needed to conceal from Naomi.

Were my instincts that professional already? Or was it something else? Sexual behavior without any genuine sexual intent or feeling often does not elicit a response. *The body knows the difference.* Mine did. What I had just witnessed was only a performance, albeit a bravura performance. I wondered what real feelings lurked behind it.

Naomi had seated herself in the metal office chair directly across from mine. Our knees were almost touching. Her posture remained provocative, her facial expression insolent. I leaned slightly forward and, as matter-of-factly as I could manage, said, "So, how are you feeling, Naomi—happy?"

Instantly her face went blank, then terrified. It was as if I had asked her the most devastating question in the world.

"God, no!" Naomi blurted, and she immediately began to cry. She bawled long and loudly, tears flooding down her cheeks, and I suddenly remembered my mathematics colleagues behind the thin walls on every side of us.

Go ahead and listen, damn you! I thought defiantly. That

sound you hear is truer than any of your calculations!
It was the sound of utter despair.

This time I *did* have to subdue a powerful natural desire: to
embrace this devastated young woman—to let her cry against
my shoulder. But of course, I followed the dicta of my training
and simply nodded sympathetically, occasionally supplying
her with a fresh tissue. When Naomi's torrent of tears finally
subsided, I asked her what it was that made her so unhappy,
and a second torrent erupted, this one of venom.

"I hate my life!" Naomi began shrilly. "I hate this goddamned school and everybody in it. Goody-goodies and po-
licemen, all trying to control me! I detest my mother and
my father and the whole goddamned neighborhood I live
in. . . ."

She went on for several minutes, the litany of malice ex-
panding to include virtually everything and everybody that
touched her life, and although her own name was missing from
the list, it was abundantly evident that above all, Naomi Goldberg hated herself.

Close to the end of the hour Naomi suddenly went quiet
and, for the first time, lowered her eyes from mine.

I waited several moments, then asked softly, "What is it,
Naomi?"

Although I was a freshman in this business, I knew that
sudden withdrawal near the end of a session sometimes sig-
nals the coming of a powerful revelation—a bombshell just
before escape.

Namoi raised her eyes but remained silent. I offered her
the thinnest possible smile of encouragement. I knew that a
gesture too large could be read as a demand, an invasion, and
she would clam up completely. Again I waited.

"I was born into the wrong family," Naomi said finally in a
low voice.

I nodded, trying not to let my disappointment show. The
"wrong family" line sounded fairly banal to me, more like a

variation on the then-popular complaint "I'm having an identity crisis!" than a bombshell revelation.

"I'm serious." Naomi went on more loudly, her eyes hard-
ening. "Somebody has made an incredible mistake."

"Exactly what kind of mistake?" I asked benignly.

"Jesus, aren't you listening to me?" Naomi barked. "I said I
was born into the wrong family!"

"You mean, you think you were adopted?" I ventured.

"God, no! *It goes back much further than that!*" Naomi said,
obviously annoyed by the banality of my response. "It's a much
bigger mistake than that!"

I was completely perplexed: "further back than that"?
Whatever could she mean? And was now the right moment to
press the question further?

The buzzer sounded, signaling the arrival of my next patient. I was reprieved.

Naomi stood, picked her sweater off the floor, and slung it
over her shoulder, then opened my cubicle door and sashayed
out. In the doorway of the cubicle next to mine, my woolly-
haired mathematician neighbor gazed at her slinking by in
her leotard, his jaw sagging. At that instant Naomi stopped,
pivoted at the waist, and smiled seductively at me.

"Same time next week?" she intoned, her dark eyes
flashing.

I nodded.

Looking utterly scandalized, the mathematician hurriedly
closed his door.

There is magic in the first encounter with a patient; you
get a slice of everything to come. In just fifty minutes I had
witnessed both Naomi's flamboyant femme fatale persona and
the pathologically low self-esteem that lurked just beneath
it, both her shamelessness and her shame, and even, in her
"incredible mistake" remark, a hint of her overwhelming desire somehow to escape from herself. It seemed a reasonable

guess that Naomi had constructed her brazen exterior as a protective response to traumatic rejection as a child.

The next time Naomi came to see me, she made another dramatic entrance—a double twirl through the door before alighting gracefully on the metal seat across from me. She was again wearing a black leotard and tights, this time overlaid with a man's white shirt open to the waist, where it was tied bolero-style. There was no "striptease" this time—a good thing, too: I didn't have unlimited confidence in the discrimination of my body's responses.

She was eager to get right down to business, to tell all. All it took was this and the following two sessions for me to put together a fairly detailed picture of how Naomi Goldberg had developed into such a painfully unhappy young woman.

Naomi had indeed been mercilessly rejected by her mother, a seamstress named Miriam. Everything about Miriam's one and only child displeased and disappointed her, starting with Naomi's sex (Miriam had "prayed" for a son, but God had "punished her" with a daughter) and her physical appearance (Miriam could never forgive Naomi for being so "swarthy." If she had to have a girl, couldn't she at least be "blond and blue-eyed"?). This latter was just one example of the mother's wholesale rejection of her own—and hence her daughter's—heritage. Both Miriam and her husband were first-generation immigrant Ashkenazi Jews with characteristically dark hair and dark eyes. How in the world could Miriam even imagine having a blond, blue-eyed child?

A possible answer to that question—albeit totally false and irrational—came in the cruel refrain Naomi had frequently heard her mother spouting to the neighbors ever since she was a toddler: "She's no child of mine, that one; we found her on the doorstep!"

Above all, Miriam condemned Naomi's behavior; she was appalled by the fact that Naomi could never act like "a proper young lady." Naomi was constantly being chastised for being too jumpy, too fidgety. She could never just walk but had to skip and dance; she could never talk softly and demurely as a young girl should but had to screech and babble and sing and swoon. Again, their ethnic heritage was an issue here.

"[Mother] always complains that I talk like an immigrant," Naomi told me. "That I use my hands too much and talk too loudly. Like a Jew, she says. I talk too much like a Jew."

By the time she was ten, Naomi was an inveterate tomboy. She wore pants—extremely rare for girls in those years—and often hid her hair under a cap. She played stickball, rode a bicycle, sneaked into movies, and got into street fights with boys her age in their lower-class neighborhood. Her mother was outraged.

"That's when she started telling me I was crazy," Naomi told me. "All the time—'You're crazy! You belong in a nut-house!' "

Of all the verbal abuse her mother hurled at her, this stung Naomi the most.

Throughout her childhood Naomi found solace in books and in the occasional Sunday company of her father. She read precociously and voraciously. *The Arabian Nights* was a special favorite. She also recalled another book that she read over and over at the age of ten: it was the true account of a Belgian Jewish girl who spent the war posing as a Catholic in a convent school.

Naomi's father, Carl, a waiter in a delicatessen, was a weak man totally intimidated by his wife. On Sundays, his one day off, he would often take Naomi away from the house, fishing and hiking. On a few of these occasions Naomi was mistaken for a boy by other fishermen; her father got a big kick out of this bit of mistaken identity and gave Naomi a boy's name, "Tony," to keep the ruse up when this happened. Naomi recalled these Sunday excursions with bittersweetness, for her father abruptly withdrew from her when at the age of twelve she began to develop sexually. He acted as though she'd suddenly become repulsive. The Sundays of solace came to an end.

Now, when Naomi would dance about the apartment with her young breasts bouncing under her sweater, her mother had a new epithet for her: "Whore!" At the time Naomi literally did not know what the word meant, but defiantly—and quite deliberately, she recalled—Naomi went straight from being a tomboy to a bombshell, dressing as provocatively as possible. Men began to stare at her, to whistle and make suggestive remarks.

"I loved it from the start," she told me. "Loved the commotion I made. Loved the power it gave me."

She also admitted to loving the way other women reacted to her. Naomi reserved a special contempt for these women.

"All those good girls in their tight brassieres looking at me from the corners of their eyes as if I'm scum—they have no idea how *numb* they are inside! How *dead!*"

But at home her father, too, had taken to calling Naomi a whore, and it hurt so much that she frequently cried herself to sleep. Sometimes the torment was so intense that she felt as if she were "cracking up inside." Soon the manner in which all men responded to her sexiness could prompt bouts of self-disgust. Still, she'd be damned if she'd give in to anyone—least of all to her mother—and behave like a "little lady."

"I'd rather die!" she declared to me.

Naomi's first sexual relationship was with a married man when she was fifteen. Since then she'd had several affairs, all of which she claimed to have enjoyed—up to a point.

"They were short and passionate, the way affairs are supposed to be," she told me. "Of course, they all ended the same way—when the guy would try to put me on a leash. First men want you because you're sexy. Then after they've got you, they want you to act like a prim little pussycat. They get jealous and mean. Or worse, they get jealous and pathetic."

Unsolicited, Naomi reported to me that she reached climax easily in intercourse, usually several times.

In these succeeding few sessions Naomi had not again alluded to the notion of being "born into the wrong family," though I found myself thinking about that line from time to time. I decided that she'd revealed more by it than I'd originally given her credit for, that it was an expression of all the rejection she'd endured growing up, a deeply felt metaphor that helped her make sense of her emotional abuse and abandonment. I imagined that it was a conscious and perfectly harmless "safety valve" fantasy that allowed her occasionally to escape the pain of that rejection: "I am not really an ugly and awful daughter, I'm just in the wrong family"—like the ugly duckling in Hans Christian Andersen's story that turns out to be "a very fine swan indeed." I did not attach any more importance to it than that.

At the beginning of our fifth session Naomi strode unceremoniously to her chair, sat down, looked earnestly into my eyes, and said, "I have something important to tell you, Akeret: I am not who you think I am."

I raised my eyebrows inquiringly.

"I'm Isabella Cortez de Seville," Naomi said. "Actually, the Contessa Cortez."

I searched her eyes for a wink or a twinkle, any clue that she was playing with me again. Nothing.

"At least that is who I was in the eighteenth century," Naomi went on. "You know, before the mistake."

I could guess, of course, what "mistake" she was referring to: being born the child of Carl and Miriam Goldberg in The Bronx.

I smiled benignly, but my pulse accelerated.

"The moment this woman—this clairvoyant I met in Greenwich Village—told me who I really was, I knew it was true. The whole thing just fit. Of course, I am an aristocrat—or at least I *was* an aristocrat until I was kidnapped."

I clung to my smile as Naomi went on to explain that as a

beautiful young contessa she had been carried away by Gypsies. Fascinating, I thought—an escape fantasy within an escape fantasy. Perhaps that was the result of a hidden fear that the first fantasy would not hold, that it needed a safety fantasy to fall back on when reality threatened to puncture it. In any event I was fairly sure this was a sign that Naomi felt her fantasies were vulnerable. As if reading my mind, she shot me a hard, critical look.

"That's who I really am, Akeret! This—" She gestured at herself with both her hands. "This really is an awful mistake, and I've got to do something about it before it's too late. I have to get back to the real me."

There was not a doubt in my mind that at some conscious level Naomi believed everything she had told me. I still hadn't uttered a word.

"You think I've got a mental problem, don't you?" Naomi suddenly blurted, her eyes wide. "You think I'm screwy, don't you?"

I swallowed hard. There are standard professional options for handling this question. I could remain silent. I could bounce the question back to her: "What do you think, Naomi? What makes you wonder if you have a mental problem?" Or, "What exactly do you mean by 'screwy'?" I could ask her how the question made her feel or if the question elicited any specific memories (of course, it did). In short, I could legitimately respond in any number of ways except by answering the question directly.

"Tell me, Akeret! I need to know," Naomi said beseechingly.

"Of course, you're not screwy," I replied with an easy smile. "Lots of people believe in reincarnation."

With that, Naomi let loose a marvelous, musical laugh, and tears of relief appeared in her eyes. I was absolutely sure I had given her the only response I could have and still retained a trusting, therapeutic relationship with her; any other response would have cast me in the same role as her mother, whose ultimate control over Naomi was to threaten her sense of sanity.

But suddenly I was overtaken by panic. My God, what had I done—traded in a rare opportunity to help my patient test her sense of reality for the short-term satisfaction of her trust and gratitude? Wasn't I, in effect, encouraging a possibly dangerous fantasy rather than helping Naomi examine it for what it was?

"Of course, who you were in an earlier life is quite a different story from who you are now," I said evenly.

"*Who I am now?*" Naomi snorted, her face gone hard and sullen again. "You mean this cesspool? This life of endless shit?"

Before I could pursue the thought any further, another tirade of pain and bitterness came gushing forth, and I decided it was best to leave the challenge alone for the time being. Anyhow, I reminded myself, believing in reincarnation doesn't necessarily make one any more deluded than, say, believing in an afterlife. And more to the point, the very fact that Naomi was continuing to rant about the pain of her Bronx childhood proved how very real that part of her life was to her.

It was during this same session that Naomi recalled how, when she was just a toddler, her mother would often flounce around the apartment bare to the waist, proudly wagging her large breasts back and forth. Miriam would do this only when her husband was out and she and Naomi were alone. One day years later, after Naomi had begun to develop sexually, she deliberately imitated her mother, dancing around the apartment with her young breasts exposed.

"[Mother] slapped me hard across the face—four or five times," Naomi told me. "And with every slap she said it again: 'Whore!' 'Whore!' 'Whore!' 'Whore!' "

This child had been punished for being a girl instead of a boy, then for being a boyish girl, and finally for being a sexy young woman. There was no way for her to win. And on top of all these confusing and abusive messages, Naomi had clearly been "commissioned" to act out her mother's secret sexual desires, which obviously included exhibitionism. I remember thinking what a wonder it was that for all of these burdens and in spite of all her difficulties in relationships, Naomi seemed basically secure in her sexual identity and in her sexuality.

Toward the end of the hour Naomi gave me a sidelong glance, then started to giggle.

"Hey, I thought you were supposed to be giving me vocational guidance in here," she said.

"What did you have in mind?"

"Well, in case you're interested, I just started taking dance lessons."

"Sounds like fun," I said. "Ballet?"

"Flamenco," Naomi replied. She suddenly stood, raised both her hands above her head in a graceful arc, snapped her fingers, threw back her head, and laughed. Then she strode out of my cubicle.

Above all, I knew I had to help Naomi rebuild her ravaged ego. I figured if we could rescue her self-esteem, she would no longer feel the need to escape into fantasies of contessas and Gypsies. I would not have to risk alienating Naomi by trying to disabuse her of any fantasy identity because that identity would simply fade away on its own once she felt better about being herself. Certainly she might continue to hate her family and regret her personal circumstances, but she would not need to see them as some kind of cosmic mistake that required a magical solution.

So over the next three months I encouraged Naomi to keep focusing on all the abuse and rejection she had endured as a child and continued to endure at home as a young woman. She was furious and rightly so, and she knew I put no limits on her expression of this fury. She could scream, she could cry, she could talk filth—and I would still be there. I was the parent

who would *never* reject her no matter how hard she tried to
shock me.

Whenever I could, I would point out how Miriam's rejection of Naomi had translated into Naomi's own low opinion of
herself and ultimately into her self-hatred. I carefully led Naomi back to rediscover her feelings as a small child hearing
her mother berate her dark hair and complexion. Naomi reex-
perienced the way she would automatically incorporate Miriam's contempt for her appearance into her own perception of
herself; it literally transmogrified the image she saw in her
mirror.

Gradually I began to weave in evidence that Miriam herself
was riddled with self-hate, that, for example, Miriam's contempt for her daughter's appearance was the result of her
warped perceptions of *herself*. We began to see that Miriam's
self-hate was in turn born of her *own* rejection as a child, that
Miriam rejected in Naomi what she had learned to hate about
herself.

"It's an ugly legacy she's passed on to you," I told Naomi
one day. "Shame begets shame. It's like a bad seed that gets
passed from one generation to another."

"How in the name of God do you break the chain?" Naomi
asked.

"We're doing it right now," I replied.

In fact, Naomi *was* changing. By her own account, she was
beginning to feel happier more of the time; she'd finally made
some friends in school, people she felt she could talk to; she
was having fewer crying jags, fewer bouts of depression and
self-loathing. And although the battles at home continued to
blaze daily, Naomi said they did not make her "go crazy" as
often as they once had. She recounted how she had recently
come home from a date at three in the morning to be met at
the door by her father, who'd spit in her face, once again calling her a whore.

"I started to cry, like always," Naomi told me. "And I started to scream at him, but suddenly it was like I was watching the whole scene from the ceiling and there was this broken man spitting and sputtering because he was so terribly unhappy and lonely. It was sad, very sad, but it didn't hurt me anymore because it had nothing to do with me."

Naomi was also forging ahead in school. She had advanced to the highest level in Spanish language, and this in turn had qualified her for a graduate course in Spanish literature and culture. She was now taking dance three afternoons a week, waitressing evenings in a Village coffee shop to cover the cost of her lessons. Now, more often than not, she wore a skirt and sweater over her leotard. She didn't mention contessas or Gypsies again the entire spring.

One morning, as I was arriving at work, Dr. Briscoe, the supervisor of student counseling, stopped me at the door to the mathematics building.

"I've been meaning to congratulate you, Robi," he said. "You've done marvelous work with that Goldberg girl."

"Thank you," I said, the young novice ever grateful for a compliment.

"Yes," Briscoe went on, thumping me on the back. "She's finally starting to act like a proper young lady."

I remember turning away from Briscoe with a sickening feeling in my stomach. I felt as if I'd betrayed Naomi, although in truth I couldn't have said exactly *how* I'd betrayed her. I said nothing more to Briscoe. I pushed the incident from my mind as quickly as I could. It was 1957. I was thirty.

In mid-June, after I had been seeing Naomi for more than six months, she came to her last appointment for the term looking disheveled and miserable. Her hair was uncombed, her face bare of makeup, her eyes bloodshot and red-rimmed. She slumped into her chair.

It seems she had decided to go to Mexico for the summer

with a girl friend from the Spanish Club. They planned to go by bus and stay in a dormitory at a Mexican school that had an affiliation with City College. But Miriam had refused to sign the requisite permission slip.

"So, now you're going south of the border to do your whoring!" Miriam had screamed. "Not with my permission!"

They'd had a knock-down, drag-out fight, more brutal than ever, and at the end Naomi had stormed out the apartment door, saying she was going to Mexico whether or not Miriam signed the slip.

"[Miriam] screamed, 'If you go to Mexico, don't think you're coming back here! You don't live here anymore! *You're no child of mine!'*

"And I screamed back, 'You'll never see me again!' "

Naomi trembled as she recounted the incident. She had to stop several times, overcome by tears. Her battered ego was struggling.

I sometimes think of the ego in physiological terms, a sort of psychic muscle that responds to training with increased strength and durability. Over the months I'd watched Naomi's ego grow tougher, more resilient. And indeed, as this session progressed, her ego began to reassert itself. Near the end of the hour Naomi suddenly smacked her hands together and declared that she should have broken away from home long ago.

I applauded Naomi's conclusion. Ideally a patient does not make major life changes in the midst of therapy, but this one was thrust upon Naomi and could, it seemed, very well advance the goal of emotional detachment from her parents.

"Actually, sometimes the best way to leave home is to leave home," I said, and Naomi smiled.

I would have liked to schedule a few more sessions with Naomi before she left in order to help her adjust to her new status, but she was departing New York in a matter of days. We made a date for her to see me at my home office as soon as she returned in late August. I walked her to the door of my cubicle and let her go.

"Have a wonderful time in Mexico," I said.

Naomi thanked me and started to slouch slowly away when the door to the next cubicle opened and my woolly-haired mathematician neighbor appeared in his doorway. Suddenly Naomi spun at the waist, threw back her head, and smiled voluptuously at me.

"*Adios, Roberto,*" she called.

THE SUN WAS JUST DROPPING below the horizon when I turned off Interstate 95 in Richmond, Virginia. I checked into a Holiday Inn and found an old-style "chop suey" Chinese restaurant where I slipped into a red vinyl banquette in the rear of the dining room. To me, eating alone in a restaurant is one of the great solitary pleasures, albeit one that my daughters tell me is not as easily enjoyed by women.

Over my egg rolls I started to read an article that a friend had cut out for me from the *Village Voice*. It described two psychologists from my alma mater, Columbia, who had "discovered" a disorder that they called Parental Alienation Syndrome, a pathology in which mothers brainwash their children against their fathers. The article said that lawyers in custody cases were now citing this syndrome as a counterpunch on behalf of fathers accused of sexually molesting their children. But another doctor, the chair of the American Psychiatric Association's Committee on Women, called the syndrome "frightening made-up psychiatry" that took a woman's normal feelings toward her ex-husband and turned them into a mental disorder—a *female* mental illness. I put the article away when my shrimp arrived.

Late that evening, after I had turned off the light and lay with my eyes open in my motel room bed, I suddenly recalled an incident that I had not thought about in thirty-five years.

It was spring. Naomi's session was my last of the day, so at its conclusion I walked out of my cubicle with her. At the door to the building we saw that it was pouring outside and Naomi asked me for a lift to the subway. I panicked, terrified that someone from the counseling office would see her getting into my car with me. To give any patient a ride would go against professional protocol; with Naomi, in particular, my peers were bound to draw sexual conclusions. But the look in Naomi's eyes was anything but sexual; it was the pleading look of a plaintive child. She was testing me. I refused. And Naomi stalked off into the rain, tossing her long mane of black hair defiantly behind her.

I slept poorly in my Richmond motel room and was back on the interstate by daybreak.

NAOMI DID NOT keep her August appointment with me. Then, late one evening in September just before fall term began, the phone in my apartment office rang.

"Robert Akeret here."

"Hello, Roberto." A woman's voice, coy, musical, with a strong Spanish accent.

"Naomi?"

"This is Isabella."

I sat down in my desk chair.

"So, how was Mexico?" I asked as calmly as I could.

"*¡Fantástico!*" Naomi replied.

"I'll want to hear all about it," I said, opening my appointment book.

But Naomi's response came back in a pell-mell monologue that I didn't dare interrupt. The trip to Mexico had been the most wonderful experience of her life, she told me in a bright and bouyant, heavily accented voice. She loved the people in her village, the food, the music. She had danced flamenco every night in a local café. She had had a marvelous love affair with a toreador. By going to Mexico she had finally come home, she said.

"That's terrific, Naomi," I interjected finally.

"My name is Isabella," she replied matter-of-factly, as though I had simply mistaken her for someone else.

"Yes, yes, Isabella," I stammered. "Let's make an appointment, okay?"

"I am not going back to the college."

"You can come to my office here," I said, adding quickly, "No charge."

"It would be wonderful to see you, Roberto," she said gaily, "but I am so busy these days. I am moving in with a friend. I am dancing in a club. I will call you as soon as I am settled, no?"

"But let's make an appointment *now*, okay, *Isabella?*"

"I will call you, Roberto. *Más tarde!*" She laughed and hung up the phone. I pictured her taunting smile as she danced away from me.

I sat alone in my office for close to an hour trying to make sense of my conversation with Naomi. What in God's name had happened to her? Was she simply "high" on her Mexican adventure? Just playing with this Spanish identity the way a teenager tries on different hats and speech patterns to see how they feel?

Or had she slipped into a full-scale delusionary disorder?

She had sounded adamant about the name Isabella, the name that a seer once told her had been her "real" name in a previous life. And her accent was not simply playful; it clearly inhabited her voice.

Still, didn't I have a friend who'd spent two years in London and come back to the States with a British accent—half assimilation, half affectation?

But Naomi had been in Mexico for less than two months and the accent overlaid her native language with the cadences of a language she'd only recently acquired.

What worried me most was that Naomi had said that going to Mexico was coming home. It sounded dangerously as if she'd finally bought into her fantasy identity. Maybe we hadn't driven it out of business after all. Maybe all our work rebuilding her ego had gone for naught.

But then why had she phoned me? She clearly did not want to dissociate herself from me completely. Was the call a cry for help? An entreaty to pull her back before she lost touch with reality altogether? *Before she went "screwy"?*

Three weeks passed without another call from her. One day between patients I phoned information to see if there were any new listings for a Naomi Goldberg. There were not. How about for an Isabella Cortez? Again, none. I considered trying to discover which Manhattan nightclubs featured flamenco dancers; there couldn't be that many of them. I could stroll casually into the one where Naomi was dancing, just another paying customer. Of course, that would have been against all professional protocol. But one more week and I would have done it.

The doorman's buzzer sounded in my apartment.

"Yes?"

"A, uh, lady to see you, Doctor," the doorman's voice said. "She says she doesn't have an appointment. Says she doesn't need one."

I looked at my watch. It was just past 9:00 P.M.

"Did she give her name?"

"Cortez. Isabella Cortez."

"Send her up."

I waited behind the door to the hallway, listening for the elevator. In a moment it was there. I heard the brittle click of heels approaching the door. I swung the door open.

Naomi stood before me in a flame red sleeveless dress that clung to her body from her neck to just above her knees, where it abruptly flared out in tiers of white taffeta ruffles. The neckline dipped precipitously between her breasts, the curve unbroken from cloth to glistening skin. Her hair—silkier than I remembered it—was parted in the middle, framing her face in an inverted V to her cheekbones, where it swung up on top of her head like a crown. Fastened at the crest was a large white gardenia.

"*¡Hola, Roberto!*" Her black eyes flashed. Her smile was electric.

"What a lovely surprise," I responded lamely.

I felt myself flushing. There was no denying it; her sexuality was unnerving me this time. There was something different about it now; it seemed infinitely more confident.

"Let's go into my office," I said.

She followed me in, and I closed the door. The obligatory couch was there, more a metaphor for the work I do than a piece of furniture I use. The walls were off-white, French doors leading to the terrace were surrounded by plants and flanked by two comfortable chairs. I gestured to one, sat in the other. Naomi smiled and alighted on the arm of the chair across from me.

"I can only stay for a moment," she said. "I have much to do. I am sailing for Seville tomorrow. But I had to see you, Roberto. To say good-bye. To say thank you."

Her accent was as pronounced as it had been on the phone, but it was her gestures that astonished me now. Her hands and arms, her face and eyes were in constant motion as she spoke. She had always been dramatic, but now her expressiveness had a specific character. In fact, voice, dress, and gesture were all one: Naomi Goldberg had completely transformed into a young Spanish woman.

It occurred to me that if Miriam Goldberg were to see her daughter now, she could no longer accuse her of "speaking like a Jew." No, not a Jew—a Spaniard. For the moment I considered the idea that perhaps Naomi was not very different from thousands of other second-generation Jews who sought assimilation in America by anglicizing their names and altering their faces with plastic surgery. That, too, was escapism, probably also born to some degree of self-hate. But did that make it pathological? Delusionary?

Didn't every successful immigrant take on the colorations of his adopted culture? And not just immigrants, but those domestic visionaries who could imagine themselves in a higher stratum of their own society and who started on their way by aping the dress and manners of the class they aspired to—until some of them actually *arrived* in that class. Certainly those people had had purists to contend with, too, relatives and friends who cried, "Don't forget who you really are!"

Was that my mission with Naomi? To cry the psychotherapeutic equivalent of "Don't forget who you really are!"?

*But my God, Naomi had completely metamorphosed overnight!*

The question was: Had she willfully reinvented herself, like an actor or a spy? Or had reality finally become so painful for her that she had fallen under the thrall of a delusion? And if a delusion, was it a simple one or a full-fledged delusionary disorder?

I have always been of the opinion that everyone is entitled to a simple delusion or two—that, say, a man who has gone half bald is permitted to convince himself that he has a full head of hair. No harm done. He is no danger to himself or anyone else.

But a delusionary disorder is an altogether different matter. It is considered a paranoid state that, if left untreated, often ends in total estrangement from reality. According to standard diagnostic criteria, Naomi's symptoms suggested that she had "delusions of a grandiose identity." One clue to this diagnosis was that the onset had been sudden, quite possibly an acute reaction to loss; after all, Naomi had in effect lost her family. But just how grandiose was it to believe that she was a young Spanish woman named Isabella? If Naomi had come in claiming to be Mary, mother of God, I probably would not have hesitated to peg her as delusional. But Isabella Cortez?

Could it be, I wondered, that Naomi was *almost conscious*

of inventing her new identity, but *not quite?* That at some level she knew that if she were to allow herself to be *fully conscious* of her impersonation, she could not pull it off? I once heard an actor say that he could give a convincing performance of a character only if he willfully suspended his disbelief that he *actually was* that character.

*But if one's performance is one's entire waking life, at what point does that willful suspension of disbelief become delusion?*

And again, if a delusion, how serious? How dangerous?

There is a murky sea lying between simple delusion and delusionary disorder. As would forever be the case for me, the finely wrought categories of my profession's diagnostic criteria did not seem to describe my patient adequately.

"I have brought you a gift, Roberto," Naomi said. "I will forever be grateful to you."

"Grateful?"

"Oh, yes! Do you forget how miserable I was when I first met you? You saved my life, Roberto."

My head was spinning.

"What do you plan to do in Seville?" I asked.

"To dance. I have a wonderful offer with the Ballet Nacional de España."

I cocked my head to one side skeptically.

*"Really?"*

"Yes, *really.*" Naomi laughed. "It is not a thing to joke about, eh? I auditioned for the director last week. He took me on the spot. I am leaving tomorrow."

Intuitively I knew she was telling the truth. I took a deep breath. I was running out of time.

"Did the director have to believe you were Spanish for you to get the job?" I asked deliberately.

"I *am* Spanish," Naomi replied, her dark eyes flashing.

"In a former life, perhaps," I said softly.

*"In this life!"* Naomi snapped. *"I have never been more myself, Roberto!"*

"It's what you've become, yes." I pushed on gently. "But of course, you started out as Naomi—"

"*I know who I am!*" she cried. "*I am Isabella Cortez!*"

She was suddenly on her feet, directly in front of me. She raised both her hands above her head and slapped them together sharply.

"This is my gift," she whispered.

I did not say a word. I did not move.

She slapped her hands together again, then again and again in acceleration. Suddenly a throaty wail pierced the air like the sound of a child crying in pain, like the sound of woman calling to her lover. For a split second I worried that my wife and daughter could hear her cry through the walls in our apartment, but I dropped that thought immediately. The wail soared higher and higher, then wavered and stopped as suddenly as it had started. Now, from seemingly out of nowhere, there were castanets rattling under Naomi's fingers as she fluttered her hands down along the sides of her breasts to her hips. She threw back her head, smiled radiantly, and stamped her feet. She was dancing for me. My gift. The flamenco.

Dance, my teachers said, is sublimation, a creative stand-in for powerful natural drives. It releases these drives without causing harm. It is what separates us from the beasts; it makes the base sublime.

Naomi was dancing her psychological history right in my office. As she swung by, I saw her as a pubescent girl mimicking her mother's bare-breasted exhibitions in their apartment—the dance that had racked her mother with shame and rage. Now, as Naomi extended her arms in front of her, I saw her dancing for her father, trying to draw him back to her, entreating him to love her as a young woman and not only as his Sunday tomboy. And now, her long arms parting in front of her, I watched Naomi gaze down at her body and proudly acknowledge that she was indeed a beauty after all. She raised her hands above her head, her face flushing. This dance was a presentation of her voluptuousness, an invitation to take sensual pleasure in it, all without shame. Her whole face declared that she loved sex, loved the feel of it. The accelerating beat of her castanets drilled the rhythms of sex into the air.

I suddenly realized that my own face was flushing. I was warm, sweating. My guard had slipped. Her sexual intent was real, and my body knew it. But never mind, I told myself, I can ride with this feeling a little longer. I am in control.

Naomi's eyes locked on mine. She danced up to me, her torso swaying. The ruffles of her dress slapped against my calves. Her arms reached down to me, beckoned to me. I smiled up at her, hesitated a second, then lifted my hands to hers. Yes, I will dance with you, Naomi/Isabella. I will celebrate your success with you. I will accept your gift of gratitude.

But the instant my hands touched hers, Naomi brushed them away and laughed—a deep-throated, haughty laugh. She stamped her feet, threw back her head, and danced away from me, spinning, laughing, her hands swaying above her head.

I sat there stunned, my face burning. My God, this whole situation was ridiculously unprofessional! It had gotten out of hand, and it was entirely my fault. By passively sitting here while Naomi danced, I was tacitly sanctioning a potentially dangerous delusion. It was my responsibility to stop her, to force her to confront reality right now.

*But I did not say a word.*

I am not entirely sure now what I had intended to say to Naomi at that point. Maybe *"Sit down! We have work to do!"* or the like. But some deep good sense made me shut up. At that moment I realized that my motive was not therapeutic at all. No, what I wanted to do was punish Naomi—for teasing me, for humiliating me, for making me lose control of myself. Above all, I wanted to strip her of her sexual power. In short, I wanted to do to her exactly what Dr. Briscoe had commissioned me to do to her.

I took a deep breath and let it out slowly, then leaned back in my chair and watched Naomi dance on. Oh, yes, this was what flamenco was all about. This was the flamenco of Carmen, a dance of seduction and rejection, of flagrant sexuality and fierce independence. It was the proud and haughty dance of a wildly sexual woman who will not be tamed. I could see now that Naomi's dance was much more than a symbolic recapitulation of her personal history; it was the history of the sexes—Man and Woman's eternal dance of approach and avoidance, of will to dominance and will to independence.

Naomi stamped her feet, a defiant staccato. I gazed at her in utter admiration. It took Naomi's passion and rage to express the soul of flamenco. She was in possession of far more of each of these than any of the young women I had seen so far in my practice. She *dared* to possess more passion and rage; that was her gift. As I watched Naomi dance, there was no doubt in my mind that she was endowed with more radiance, more power, more life energy as a young Spanish dancer than she had ever possessed as the desperately unhappy daughter of Miriam and Carl Goldberg from The Bronx.

Perhaps, I thought, she was not caught in a delusion of any kind. Perhaps, in some transcendent sense, she *had* been born into the wrong family.

Perhaps it was true that Naomi Goldberg had changed her identity in order to become her true self.

"O body swayed to music, O brightening glance / how can we know the dancer from the dance?"

The stamping stopped. The dance was over. I rose to my feet and applauded.

"You are magnificent, Isabella," I said.

"Oh, thank you, Roberto," she replied.

She rushed up to me and kissed my cheek. There were tears in her eyes.

"Tell me, Isabella, are you happy?"

A wonderful, musical laugh erupted from her throat.

"Oh, God, yes, Roberto. *Very!*"

A moment later I let her out the door.

That was thirty-five years ago.

I had not seen Isabella since, but I had never stopped think-ing about her, never stopped worrying that in my youthful naïveté I had allowed her to go out unprotected into the treach-erous realities of the rest of her life.

MY FRIEND Ben Rose, a private investigator, told me how to track down Naomi/Isabella on my computer in ten minutes flat.

"Two names makes it cinchy," he'd said.

I'd called Isabella the same day I found her number.

"Poodles" was the way she answered the phone.

I said who I was. She laughed and said, "I was thinking about you just yesterday, Robi."

*Robi*, not *Roberto*. Nor did I detect an accent. Yet that musi-cal voice was unmistakable.

I did not want either of us to exchange much over the phone, so I immediately began telling her about the pilgrim-age I was planning. But the moment the word *follow-up* came out of my mouth, I felt a throb of embarrassment.

"It's more of a personal thing really," I went on quickly. "I don't want to intrude in any way."

"Don't be silly," Isabella had chimed. "I can't wait to see you."

She'd given me directions to her place in a neighborhood of Miami known as Little Havana.

"Number Six Twenty-nine Calle Ocho—Eighth Street," she'd said. "I'm usually in my shop during the day."

Three days and two nights after I left New York, I crossed the border into Florida. I put Mozart on the tape deck for the final hundred miles of my journey; it seemed the farthest I could get from Isabella. I wanted her voice and image out of my mind so I could come upon her fresh, not overwhelmed by my memory of her. But it was no help; Isabella's image kept pushing through the Mozart. By the time I rolled into Miami, I'd given up and put on Miles Davis one more time.

THE CORAL PINK SIGN in the window of 629 Calle Ocho read, THE PAMPERED POODLE. I shaded my eyes and looked in through the glass.

Stacked along the nearest wall were three tiers of steel cages, each one housing a fluffy, freshly laundered poodle. I could hear them yapping through the window. Along the back wall was a wide counter, and in the far corner, perched on a high stool reading a book, was Isabella.

She wore a white off-the-shoulder peasant blouse that exposed two or three inches of her bosom. She had on black spandex pants that stopped just below her knees. Her hair was tied back from her face in a turquoise scarf. Even from this distance I could see that her dark eyes still sparkled. She looked as if she were in her thirties—thirty-five at most. I knew that she was fifty-three years old.

I stood there a few seconds, studying her. I often wish I could spy on my patients when they think they are alone and unseen, when they have no reason to project an image of themselves. It is not that I think of this solo self as *truer* than any of their other selves, but it is a self I rarely get to glimpse, a piece of the puzzle I usually have to infer from my patients' self-conscious reports. Isabella looked bright, expectant, full of life. And in that she seemed totally peaceful and unafraid sitting there in her poodle parlor, she looked remarkably innocent to me.

Suddenly I felt like backing away from the window and racing back to my car before she could see me. She's obviously fine, I thought. Not only has she survived, but she looks healthy and happy. Don't mess with it, I said to myself. I have no business being here. What if my presence brings back dangerous thoughts? What if I upset her lovely equilibrium?

"Robi! It's you!" She was off her stool, striding to the shop door and opening it. "I wondered who that handsome gentleman was sneaking looks at me!"

She danced lightly up to me and kissed my cheek. I grinned and shook my head: thirty-five years in the blink of an eye.

"You look wonderful," I said. It was true; she looked even younger close up.

"Let me lock up. We'll have tea upstairs," she said.

"I don't want to disturb your normal day."

"I haven't had a normal day in my life!" She laughed. "You, of all people, should know that, Robi!"

That throaty laugh had not aged either.

She turned the cardboard sign in the door to CLOSED / CERRADO and led me up an outdoor stairway to the front door of the blue stucco house above the shop. The rooms were bright and colorful, the walls lined with shelves crammed with books in both English and Spanish. This, too, is a privilege I wish I could be granted with all my patients: to view their living spaces, to see the parts of their personalities that decorate the walls. At the head of the living room was a large framed poster of Isabella in full flamenco regalia, her arms gracefully arced over her head. I could not say how old she was in the picture.

I sat down on a rattan sofa directly under the poster. Isabella made us tea, then sat down at the other end, her feet tucked under her.

"So, what do you want to know, Doctor?" she asked teasingly. No, there was not even a trace of a Spanish accent left in her voice.

"I want to know how you are," I said. "That mostly."

She closed her eyes and took a deep breath before replying.

"I'm good," she said quietly. "Good and happy, good and sad. You know."

I nodded. I thought for a second she might tear up, but she quickly brightened.

"Where should I begin?" she asked.

"How about when you walked out of my office that night in 1958?"

We both laughed, then both went quiet. Isabella took another deep breath and began.

"I danced with the Ballet Nacional for twelve years. It was incredible, Robi, the highest of highs. I danced, and they loved me. My picture was in the papers all the time. People in the street, they'd call out, 'Isabella! Isabella!' Being a star flamenco dancer is like being a movie star over here. I had princes chasing after me, princes and playboys. We toured everywhere: South Africa, Australia, Hawaii, all over the Continent. I loved every minute of it. After two years I was one of the premier women dancers in the company. After six I was married to the ballet orchestra's lead guitarist, Antonio."

I leaned back, smiling, as Isabella went on, regaling me with stories of her fabulous career. From time to time she would jump up, rush to another room, and return with a program or a poster or a scrapbook of newspaper clippings. Last she brought out a photo album.

"Here I am at our mansion in Seville. Sixteen rooms. Beautiful gardens, eh?" She pointed at a photograph of herself sitting on a wrought-iron chair in front of a blaze of bougainvillaea. "You would have loved that house, Robi. It was once a contessa's, can you believe that?"

I grinned in amazement—the "Contessa Isabella Cortez" at her mansion in Seville. Isabella turned the page to a photograph of the mansion's terrace. A sharp-featured man with a shock of black hair sat holding a guitar, an older woman standing behind him with one hand on his shoulder. The woman held her handsome head high, as if she were royalty. She looked remarkably like Isabella.

"Who is she?" I asked.

Isabella hesitated, her face flushing.

"It's Mother," she said finally. "She came visiting once."

I nodded.

"She read about me in the papers and sent a telegram saying how proud she was and all is forgiven, that sort of thing. In a way it was my dream come true. She said she wanted to visit, and I couldn't resist. I just had to show her my house, my husband, this whole wonderful life I had."

"And your father?"

"He was dead. He'd died a few years after I left, although I didn't hear about it until much later," she said.

"How long did your mother stay?"

Isabella shrugged. "A few weeks, I guess."

She immediately turned the page. On this one was an enlarged photograph of a group of beautiful barefoot women dancing in a village street.

"Here I am in Andalusia, dancing the real flamenco with the other Gypsies," she said cheerfully. "They couldn't believe I was actually American."

I felt a chill cross my shoulders. I looked straight into Isabella's eyes but didn't say a word.

"I never felt completely at home there, Robi." She went on rapidly, her voice lower. "The Spanish are so rigid, especially the men. They call it macho. I call it uptight. My heart bled for all the Spanish little girls, the daughters of my friends. They lock them up like silverware. No one ever takes them fishing. These poor *niñas* have two choices: to grow up to be a lady or a whore. There's nothing in between. Over there they all act so cultured, but it's just an act. They never want to know what you are really like—what's deep in your soul."

I literally held my breath. I had a hundred questions I wanted to ask Isabella at that moment, but I remained silent.

"Did you ever hear the expression 'Beware of what you desire, for you will surely get it'?" she asked.

"Yes."

"Well, that's exactly what happened to me. Everybody loved me over there. They completely accepted me as Spanish. And I *was*—I *was* Spanish for the first few years. Spanish through and through. I mean, how else could I have danced like that? I never had to work at it. It just all came naturally to me, like déjà vu. But after a while my American side rebelled. It wanted to come out again."

Isabella shrugged and smiled at me, her dark eyes gleaming.

"Your American side?" I repeated, my pulse racing.

"Yes, you know—my wild side. That part of me that won't stay still, that won't be put in a box. That's my American side. It just wouldn't be stifled, know what I mean?"

"So—so you returned to being your old self," I said, desperately trying to sound as casual as she did. "Back to your American self, Naomi Goldberg."

I watched her face intently as I said that name. She didn't bat an eyelash.

"Oh, no, it wasn't as easy as that," she replied animatedly. "It was a real struggle. A battle royal, actually. I mean, I don't know about anybody else, Robi, but I've got lots of selves inside me, all fighting to be the star. And I've always got to referee between them, pick the parts that feel right at the time. My Spanish side and my American side still get into skirmishes now and then."

Isabella cocked her head to one side.

"But isn't it wonderful, Robi? I mean, the way you can be so many people in one lifetime?"

She delivered this line with the smiling nonchalance of Shirley MacLaine on a late-night talk show.

A wild laugh burst out of me; I couldn't have held it in if I'd wanted to. So this was it, the denouement, the answer to the question that had been haunting me for all these years—all these *decades:* At fifty-three years old, Isabella Cortez, born Naomi Greenberg, in radiant good health and in possession of her own business, a fine house, and a full range of emotions, thinks it's just grand that you can pack a whole bunch of lives into one. That, in the end, was apparently the sum total of her "delusion."

My God, whatever had I been worrying about?

"What's so funny, Robi?" Isabella asked.

"Me," I replied. "Sometimes I think I make life far too complicated. I guess it comes with my line of work."

We talked on for three or four hours. She told me that when she was thirty-two, she'd left the ballet company because she wanted to leave in her prime, not as a has-been. She and Antonio had set up a dance school in London for several years, but finally she had wanted to return to America.

"I've been here since," she said. "What is it now—sixteen, seventeen years? We tried to set up a flamenco school here, too, but it didn't take. Antonio could never adjust to America anyhow, so he finally went back home to Spain. It was time. We'd had some good years together, and then it was over. I only wish we'd had a child at some point, but the timing never seemed right."

In the meantime, she'd become passionately interested in poodles and set up her own business here in Miami. She still danced occasionally at clubs and festivals. She said that she'd had several boyfriends since Antonio, but no grand passion, although currently she was seeing a man named Frederico whom she found very attractive.

Isabella's living room had gradually darkened and now was filling with pink light. Out the window I saw the sun setting in Little Havana harbor.

"What do you say I take you out to dinner?" I asked.

"Wouldn't that be lovely," she said, rising from the sofa. "I know just the spot for us."

She went into her bedroom to get ready, and when she returned minutes later, she was almost unrecognizable: She wore a blond wig with long, bouncy corkscrew curls, bright red lipstick, and black eye shadow that glittered with gold flecks. Her black dress was tight and very short, her tan legs bare.

"For some reason I feel especially sexy tonight," she said, slipping her arm through mine.

We took my van. For the first time since I arrived, we fell silent. Isabella turned on my radio, found a Spanish station playing conga music. Suddenly the front seat started bouncing. I glanced over at Isabella. Her feet were popping, her torso swaying, her shoulders gyrating; she was dancing in her seat. I smiled. *That child never could sit still.*

As we turned onto the shore drive, a shower burst overhead and rain splashed in through my open window. I found myself thinking again of the day I had refused my young patient a ride in the rain.

"Do you remember the time you asked me for a ride—"

"—to the subway?" Isabella finished my question. "Of course, I do! I hated you, Robi! I almost quit therapy right then and there."

"I had no choice, you know," I said. "It would have been unprofessional of me."

*"That's not why you did it!"* Isabella shot back.

I swallowed hard.

"No, I guess not," I said. "I was afraid of how it might look."

I glanced over at Isabella. She was staring straight through the windshield at the pouring rain.

"I'm sorry," I said softly.

Isabella shrugged and laughed. "What the hell! That was thirty-five years ago! Who cares?"

"I suppose I do," I said.

I took a deep breath before going on. I hadn't planned this, but now I knew I had to say it.

"There's something else I want to tell you, Isabella. It's about the school; they sent you to me under false pretenses."

I told her about Dr. Briscoe's note, that my real assignment had not been to give her vocational guidance but to modify her behavior in the classroom.

"It's not the first time a therapist has been enlisted to control someone. Especially to control a woman. They said your sexiness posed a threat to the school, but the truth is these guys were threatened by their own guilty drives. You represented every middle-aged man's worst fear: a woman who truly loves sex. It scares them. Hell, it scared me. We're all afraid we can't handle a woman like you, that you'll make fools of us. So we try to tame you. That was my assignment: to tame you."

"Like Carmen," Isabella murmured.

"Exactly," I said. "You were the first 'Carmen' I ever saw in my practice. But later on—in the sixties and seventies—I saw Carmens by the dozen. Women who wanted to own their sexuality without shame. Who were tired of being good little girls who had to hide their sexual appetites. It took me a long time to realize that this wasn't a neurotic symptom I was dealing with; it was a social realignment. You were ahead of your time, Isabella."

I glanced over at her. She looked upset, apprehensive.

"But none of them could dance the flamenco, could they, Robi?" she asked in an urgent, little-girl voice.

"No," I replied. "None of them could dance the flamenco."

"Well." She snorted. "They weren't really Carmens then, were they?"

"I guess not, Isabella."


We ate paella on the lantern-lit terrace of a sprawling Spanish restaurant by the sea. Inside, couples danced to marimba music. Half the men there seemed to know Isabella. They held their sangria glasses up to her as she passed by; she greeted them in Spanish.

After our coffee was served, Isabella grew quiet.

"I have a confession for you, too," she said softly a few moments later. "I didn't tell you the whole story about my mother. She didn't just visit us once and that was it. When Antonio and I came back to America, we moved in with her. And we stayed for eight years."

Oh, God, I thought, here it comes: the real follow-up story, the one I could have never guessed but always feared. I forced myself to sip my coffee quietly as Isabella told me about those eight years in her mother's house. It was awful.

She and Antonio had moved in with Miriam as a temporary measure to save money while they set up a dancing school in New York, but when that venture proved impossible, they stayed on while Isabella searched for an alternative. Isabella said that she had been confident she could handle her mother this time. She felt strong enough to hold her own after all those years of celebrity and independence. And anyway, Miriam was old and infirm and at last seemed to respect her. But little by little Isabella's return home at the age of forty turned into a nightmare reenactment of her childhood.

"Antonio was so depressed with nothing to do that all he did was hang around the apartment playing the guitar while I looked for some way for us to make a living. Pretty soon he and Miriam were drinking together, getting wrecked and smoking and watching television all day. When I'd come home from looking for work, they'd look at me all dressed up and Antonio would start swearing at me. He was convinced I'd been out whoring. It was Mother who put that idea in his head."

Isabella recounted these events in a flat, toneless voice; I'm sure it was the only way she could get it out. Several times I tried to signal her that she did not have to go on if she did not want to, but just like thirty-five years earlier, Isabella had to tell me every painful detail.

"I tried to leave hundreds of times. But Mother was getting sicker; it turned out she had bladder cancer. And I still felt responsible for Antonio; I'd brought him all the way over here. I thought of killing myself. I hadn't thought of that since I was a teenager, since I first came to see you. Since you saved my life."

She raised her large, soulful eyes to mine. Suddenly she was smiling again.

"But listen to this, Robi. . . . One day, when I thought I just couldn't take it one day more, I went into the hall closet and started meditating. I could hear them drinking and laughing in the other room. And I concentrated on one thought with all my might: *I wished they would disappear.* And they did! Two days later Mother died. And a week after that Antonio went back to Spain. It was all over. *I'd done it again!*"

A deep, earthy laugh erupted from Isabella's throat. Her eyes were sparkling again. I lifted my wineglass and smiled at her.

"Here's to you, Isabella," I said. "To one of the greatest survivors of all time."

WE DROVE BACK along the shore drive in silence.

Did those eight torturous years mean that ultimately I had failed Isabella? Clearly I had not led her far enough to avoid another long chapter of demonic entrapment by her mother, a repetition of a deeply neurotic, life-sucking pattern. That certainly did not sound like the product of successful therapy to me.

I remember reading Hegel's philosophy of history when I was a student; the philosopher saw the driving forces of history as going in cycles, from thesis to antithesis to synthesis, spiraling ever upward to higher, more complex levels of being. At forty Isabella had been a synthesis of the Bronx-born Naomi and the flamenco star Isabella whom she had become in antithesis to her original identity. Finally she had been her own creation. And that created self had once again survived her monstrous mother.

It seemed to me that Isabella was propelled by a powerful

life-force that was capable of surviving just about anything. She *was* one of the all-time great survivors. Maybe early on I had helped her nurture that life-force. Maybe I had prevented her from getting stuck in history.

Or maybe, I thought as I drove on through the night, I am just trying to justify myself.

How *do* you determine what a successful posttherapy life is? It's never happily-ever-after for anyone. This follow-up business was not going to be easy.

What, I wondered, if I had "straightened out" Naomi back in 1957? What if I had led her farther along the route to self-knowledge and self-acceptance as we interpreted those notions back then? Naomi Goldberg probably would have finished school; she might have married well, lived in the suburbs, raised children, found contentment.

*But would she have danced for princes?*

As we turned onto Calle Ocho, I saw that a man was standing in front of the stairway to Isabella's house. He was tall with slicked-back hair, good-looking, about thirty-five or forty, I guessed.

"It's Frederico!" Isabella blurted excitedly. "Isn't he gorgeous? He's going to be so jealous when he sees me with you."

I smiled. Suddenly Isabella grabbed my arm.

"Oh, Robi," she whispered urgently, "can you keep a secret?"

"Sure. What is it?"

"It's Frederico. He's kind of funny about certain things. I haven't told him everything about myself. So when you meet him, don't let on that I'm—you know."

I gazed into her worried eyes. Was the lady afraid that I would give away her age?

"That you're what?" I asked softly.

"Jewish," she whispered, looking away.

I never did meet Frederico. I dropped Isabella on the other side of the street, and we made our good-byes there.

"Won't I see you tomorrow?" she asked.

"I don't think so. I have to move on," I answered.

"Oh, Robi." Isabella sighed. "Don't you wish life just went on and on forever?"

She kissed my cheek and was gone before I could answer.

# T W O

# Charles: The Soul of Love

> The next thing then she waking looks upon,
> Be it on lion, bear, or wolf, or bull,
> On meddling monkey, or on busy ape,
> She shall pursue it with the soul of love.

William Shakespeare, *A Midsummer-Night's Dream*

INTERSTATE 75 took me northwest from Miami to Sarasota, city of 361 days of sunshine and final home of the late John Ringling, circus king. I arrived midday on a Tuesday, a full twenty-four hours before I was scheduled to meet Charles Embree, whom I'd last seen almost thirty years earlier. I was grateful to have a day to myself before reconnecting with Charles; I was still digesting my encounter with Isabella.

I checked into the Comfort Inn and took a lovely long swim in the pool before setting out to explore the town. Sarasota has architectural flourishes that give it a distinctly Mediterranean air; one sees it in the magnificent botanical garden in the heart of the city, in the grand John and Mabel Ringling Museum of Art out on Bayshore Drive, and in the elegant Ringling mansion, Ca'd'zan, modeled after the Doges' Palace in Venice. Ringling, who grew up in Baraboo, Wisconsin, with romantic dreams in his head, was naturally drawn to the splendor and decadence of Italy, where in the form of that primordial animal act that played at the Colosseum—pitting Christians against lions—it is said that the first circus was born.

After lunch of pan-seared tuna in a café overlooking the marina, I drove to the neighboring town, Venice, so named by John Ringling and the home of his training academy, Clown College. There, under a permanent big top, new acts for the Ringling Brothers and Barnum & Bailey Circus were in rehearsal. Visitors were welcome. The bleachers were nearly empty. I took a seat high above the center ring.

A curly-haired, muscular young man in tights and a tank top was hanging upside down from his trapeze as a lithe and beautiful young woman in a body-hugging costume swung through the air across from him. The sound system was playing Tchaikovsky—the final solo from *Swan Lake*. The young woman was the very embodiment of grace, a soaring ballerina. But that was not the only reason I could not take my eyes off her.

The young man was now swaying in synchronization with the young woman's movements. He was the catcher. She was soon to let go, to fly through the air at fifty feet above the ground and latch on to his outstretched arms. There was a net, to be sure, but I knew very well that she might drop wide of it onto the sawdust-covered floor or that she could come hurtling down into the net at an angle that could maim or kill her. Only a few years earlier one of the famous Flying Wallendas had met such a fate. The music swelled. I squinted in terror, my heart pounding.

The truth is some dark part of me was mesmerized by the danger, kept imagining the seductive angel missing the catcher's outstretched arms and crashing to the ground. That is the drama, the tension between success and failure that keeps all of us riveted in our seats. Clearly I would not be watching with such keen interest if the young woman were not so attractive, but I certainly would not be watching with such fascination if she were not in mortal danger, too. In the last analysis I am probably not that different from the members of Caligula's audience at the Circus Neronis who watched excitedly as naked gladiators were chased down by hungry lions. Sex and danger have always been a winning combination in show business.

The young woman swung free. She somersaulted twice in midair and then reached her arms out to the upside-down man. He caught her. I sighed with relief. No, I did not want to see her come hurtling to her death. I am not perverse.

But God help me, I wanted to see her try it again.

"ROBI, I'VE GOT a thorny case I'd like you to take a look at. Rollo thought you might be the right man for the job. Thinks it needs an unorthodox approach."

It was Dr. Goldman, head of New York University Counseling Services, on the phone. The year was 1965. I was now in private practice.

"What can you tell me about it?" I asked.

"I'd rather not say much. Let you make your own assessment. The young man's name is Charles Embree. Former college student." Goldman paused a second before adding, "He currently works in a circus."

If I had needed any further persuasion to take the case, that would have done it. I have been a circus aficionado ever since I can remember. If I find myself on a tennis court with more than two balls in hand, I invariably start juggling them—or at least I try to. And when I am riding my horse alone in the Adirondack woods, I am quite likely to drift off into a fantasy that takes me bareback to the center ring of the Schumann Circus. But the truth is I did not need any more inducement to see Charles Embree than the fact that Rollo May, the teacher whom I greatly admired, had recommended me for the job. Like almost everybody else, I have never fully outgrown my desire to live up to my "father's" expectations.

Embree first came to see me early on a Friday morning. He was a large young man with a round, shaggy-bearded face, long hair, and a rotund torso. There was a broad white bandage above his left eyebrow reaching to his hairline. He ambled up to me lugubriously, turning his head from side to side as he took in the furnishings of my office. In spite of the beard, there was something of the overgrown boy about Charles. Like many first-time male patients, he wanted to shake hands with me—a ritual whose historical origin is in checking one another for hidden weapons. His hand was surprisingly soft, his grip gentle. I gestured to the seat across from me, and we both sat down.

"So, what brings you here?" I asked mildly.

"I guess I'm having a little trouble making up my mind if I want to stick with my job," Charles replied. He looked me straight in the eye without any visible anxiety as he spoke. His voice was low, a touch gravelly but pleasant. "You know, sometimes I think I should move on to something else."

Often, in this initial minute or two with a new patient, I pick up visual or aural clues, perhaps even subliminal vibrations, that tell me in the most general terms what kind of burden he is carrying with him: a deep depression, anxiety, a focused fear. At times I have even been able to detect nonverbal signs of paranoia or of a specific phobia. But I picked up practically nothing this time—maybe just a touch of normal "Young Man's Melancholy." I nodded to Charles, encouraging him to go on.

"But I love the circus," he said with obvious enthusiasm. "I love just about everything about it—the smells, the cotton candy, the animals." He shrugged and smiled shyly. "I don't know, maybe I just never grew up. I wanted to run away to the circus ever since I was a boy, and now that I'm there, I don't really want to leave."

So far his situation sounded eminently reasonable to me. Heaven knows, I had no trouble identifying with it. In my mind I was jumping ahead, wondering what the problem could be. Did young Charles have parents with more conventional career plans in mind for him? Could this possibly be the "thorny" problem that required the intervention of an "unorthodox" therapist?

"And what's the argument against staying with the circus?" I asked.

Charles shrugged again.

"It's—it's kind of a chancy business," he said, lowering his eyes from mine.

"Chancy?"

"Well, hazardous, actually," Charles said, still not looking back into my eyes.

Aha, that was it. Charles worked in a dangerous act—the high wire, perhaps, or the trapeze. But he did not appear to have the right body type for either of those. Maybe he was the human cannonball. That line of work could make a man seriously consider a career change.

I waited. Charles sighed, dropping his woolly head lower; then he shrugged again.

"I've fallen in love with someone at work," he finally said miserably.

So, it was a hazard of a different sort—a hazard of the heart. Again I waited, but when Charles did not speak for several minutes, I prodded him with "And how is it going?"

"Up and down. Well, not very good, actually." Charles wagged his large head back and forth. Then, with a sudden burst of passion, he said, "I have never been so in love in my life, Doctor. *Never!*"

I looked at Charles sympathetically. For all the hundreds of times the broken heart of unrequited love has revealed itself to me in my office, it is always painful to behold.

"Tell me about—" I stopped myself before I had to commit to pronoun gender.

"She's an incredible beauty." Charles jumped in ardently. "Voluptuous. Intense. Provocative. I've wanted her desperately since the first time I saw her."

"And she?"

"I have to win her over. It's all I really want in life," Charles said breathlessly. "And I think I can. It's just a matter of time."

Charles was now fumbling with something in his shirt pocket. It was a photograph. He regarded it a moment with obvious fondness, then passed it to me.

The photograph showed Charles, thinner and beardless, in a circus ring standing next to a polar bear that was upright on its hind legs. For several seconds the significance of what I was looking at did not register on me. But then, when it finally did, I summoned up every ounce of self-control I had within me to smile calmly and say in a natural-sounding voice, "She's lovely."

Charles's face radiated relief. I had accepted his romance on his own terms.

"Her name is Zero," he offered in a confidential tone, as if this bit of information were a gift of gratitude.

It was then, in delayed response, that my panic set in. By every diagnostic criterion I knew, Charles was a very seriously ill young man. Furthermore, on the basis of my professional experience to date, I was not well prepared to treat such an unusual disorder. Yet Rollo May had told Dr. Goldman that he thought I was the right man for the job. I took a deep breath and regarded the love-struck young man across from me.

And then a second wave a panic swept over me. I was staring at the bandage on Charles's forehead, and I suddenly knew why his job had become so hazardous.

"Why did she scratch you?" I asked softly.

Charles looked down at the floor shame-faced.

"She wasn't ready for me," he replied in a hurt voice. "I rushed her, and she wasn't ready."

Without further prodding, Charles went on to tell me exactly how it had happened. For over a year he had been assistant to Glorious Glorianna, the woman who trained and performed with Zero. Charles had, in his words, "fallen head over heels in love" with the bear from the start but had limited his overtures to her to softly growled words of affection and pats on the animal's flank and neck when he was in the cage or performance ring with her. It was required that he wear a thick leather jacket as protection whenever he was in contact with the bear, and he did. Polar bears, Charles informed me matter-of-factly, are particularly dangerous because they are capable of killing a human with a single blow and give no warning before they strike.

On the night in question—just two weeks before Charles was referred to me—he had remained late in the animal area of the grounds where the circus was playing nearby in New Jersey. Sitting outside Zero's cage, he had guzzled down a six-pack of beer, all the while speaking softly to the bear, telling her how much he cared for her, occasionally tossing her a "bear cookie" through the bars. And then, his courage finally plucked up, he unlocked the cage door and entered, speaking words of love to Zero. She responded by immediately clubbing him on the shoulder with her right paw. Fortunately he had been wearing his leather jacket, and his only injury came from a glancing claw scratch on his forehead. It required fourteen stitches.

I listened to Charles's long narrative with the same outward calm that I had mustered when he initially revealed the identity of his beloved to me. Interestingly, it had already become somewhat easier for me to do this. Had the shock already begun to wear off? I leaned toward Charles.

"What had you hoped would happen between the two of you?" I asked.

Charles shrugged shyly. "I just wanted to show her some affection," he said. "To nuzzle with her a little bit."

"That's all?"

Charles shrugged again, but said nothing.

"Were you sexually excited?" I asked.

Charles looked back at me with an even gaze.

"Genuine affection always leads to sex, doesn't it?" he said, raising his voice in what sounded like a challenge. "That's only natural."

*Natural?* My head was spinning. It was only by transcending the very question of what is "natural" that I had been able to carry on this conversation with such equanimity.

"Natural, maybe, but it certainly does sound hazardous," I replied, offering a benign smile.

Charles hesitated; he was, I think, carefully studying my face for signs of disapproval or derision. He finally smiled back at me.

"The hazards of love." He sighed softly.

I now knew with perfect clarity that above all else, my job with Charles was to save his life, to prevent him from being crushed to death in his paramour's embrace. Whatever work we might do together would be either in service of that goal or secondary to it. In a sense that focus should have made my initial therapeutic decisions easier. It didn't.

When a patient is at risk of losing his life, by either self-destructive "accident" or willful suicide, he is automatically a candidate for incarceration in a mental institution. There he can be monitored day and night, sedated, too, if necessary. I have no doubt that incarceration can save lives and, conversely, that failing to incarcerate a patient can lead to his premature death. I know this only too well.

Three years before encountering Charles, I had been a postdoctoral fellow at a Veterans Administration psychiatric hospital. This institution was a virtual war zone between therapists who advocated a blanket use of psychotropic drugs, often in conjunction with electroshock therapy, and therapists who, like myself, thought that drugs and shock therapy should be used only after other methods—basically individual and group therapy—had been given a reasonable chance for success.

One day I was asked to evaluate a veteran with severe depression who had recently been admitted to the hospital. This young man, a second-year medical student, was terrified of electroshock therapy. He had already heard morbid jokes on the ward about one shock-happy psychiatrist who the other patients said was "trained at Con Edison." I assured the young man that I would place him in one of my therapy groups, thus guaranteeing that he would not be given shock, at least not for a very long while. I was new at this facility, and unbeknownst to me, being in a therapy group automatically conferred on a patient access to certain privileges, including weekend passes home. Knowing how seriously depressed this patient was, I never would have granted him such a pass, but my supervisor did. That very first weekend the patient went home and shot himself through the head with his father's pistol. Whatever responsibilities were or were not mine in this tragic case, I was—and remain still—haunted by that young man's suicide.

But what of this young man seated across from me who wanted to make love to a polar bear—to an unwilling mistress with lethal claws? It seemed to me that Rollo May certainly would have recommended Charles's immediate incarceration if that is what he believed should have been done. Furthermore, Charles was obviously conscious of the danger he put himself in whenever he approached Zero; he had worn his protective coat on the night of his attempted "assignation." And there was something else that figured in my deliberation: Locking Charles in an institution—in effect, caging him—might press him further into his identification with the animal. But more important than any of these considerations was the fact that Charles had voluntarily sought help. And the help that he said he wanted was in making up his mind whether or not to remain on his hazardous job. Charles was, I believe, asking me to help him save his own life. He knew very well how easily his passion could kill him.

Our fifty minutes were nearly over.

"If we are going to work together, you are going to have to make me a promise," I said.

Charles raised his eyebrows.

"You have to promise not to attempt to make love to Zero in any way until our work is over. After that you can do whatever you wish."

Charles scratched at his beard.

"Okay, I promise," he said.

"Good." At that moment I believed him.

Charles rose heavily from his chair.

"By the way, I can only see you for five weeks," he said in an offhand manner.

"Why is that?"

"Because that's when the circus leaves town."

AFTER CHARLES LEFT, I sat still for several minutes, my mind churning as I tried to make sense of Charles's predicament. What in the name of God did it mean to be in love with a polar bear? What was its emotional content? And what were Charles's emotional expectations for it? Did he really believe that his love for the animal could be reciprocated? Did reciprocation even matter?

I certainly understood what it was to have a personal relationship with a domesticated animal; I had had one with my horse when I was a boy. I knew what it was to go alone into a stable and tell my deepest secrets to a four-footed animal and to believe that the look in his eye showed that he comprehended every word I said, that he empathized with me totally. Further, I knew the comfort, even the outright sensuality, of a horse's warm nose nuzzling against my chest. I truly loved my horse; indeed, I love the horse I own today. But what Charles had described to me was love of an entirely different order. It was deep and romantic. It was an alternative to loving another human being. And yet, like the most mature interhuman love, it was a love that led "naturally" to sex.

Zoophilia, the drive to have sexual relations with animals, is a subcategory of paraphilia, so named because the deviation *(para)* lies in that to which the individual is attracted *(philia)*. Also included in this category are the more common disorders of exhibitionism, fetishism, frotteurism (compulsive "mashing" of strangers), pedophilia, sexual masochism, sexual sadism, transvestism, and voyeurism. What all these disorders have in common, the *Diagnostic and Statistical Manual of Mental Disorders* declares, is sexual arousal in response to objects or situations "that are not part of normative arousal activity patterns."

But on that day in 1965 none of the books on my shelf had an entry for "paraphilia," only for "sexual deviations and perversions." And there, listed along with pedophilia and fetishism, was an "abnormal arousal activity pattern" called homosexuality.

Incredible.

Just eight years after I first encountered Charles Embree, I would play hooky from work for a day so that I could hear Dr. Thomas Szasz speak at Cornell University. Szasz had turned the psychiatric establishment upside down with his revolutionary book, *The Myth of Mental Illness,* a brilliant deconstruction of standard psychological concepts. In it Dr. Szasz had raised that pesky question that people in my profession prefer not to think about—or at least prefer not to discuss in public: *Who decides who's crazy anyhow?*

After Szasz was introduced to the packed university hall, he took chalk in hand, walked silently to the far end of the blackboard, and jotted down the numbers "58%" and "38%" and "4%." Then he strolled back to the podium and began his lecture on the history of the concept of "mental disorder" in Western civilization. About three-quarters of an hour into his talk, Szasz reported that he had just attended the annual convention of the American Psychiatric Association and that that august body, in its collective wisdom, had come to the conclusion that it had been "wrong" about homosexuality all along— that it wasn't a "mental disorder" after all.

"And that—over there—is the breakdown of their vote," Dr. Szasz said, gesturing to the numbers he had written on the blackboard. "Fifty-eight percent voted in favor of eliminating homosexuality as a mental illness, thirty-eight percent were opposed, and four percent abstained. *Isn't democracy a marvelous thing?*"

Ten thousand, six hundred, and forty-six members had voted on the issue. The year was 1973.

Of course, in 1965 I did not have the benefit of that vote. And even if I had, even if same-gender sexual love had already crept out of the "mental disorder" closet, what implications would this have had for interspecies sexual love? Was the "abnormality" of zoophilia inherently different from the "abnormality" of homophilia? Statistically not that much; according to Kinsey, 7 percent of boys growing up on farms engage in sex with animals.

There was one intriguing clue in the general definition of perversion offered in the *Diagnostic Manual*. It said that these disorders "in varying degrees may interfere with the capacity for *reciprocal, affectionate activity.*" Indeed, that was certainly a serious problem for Charles with Zero.

But that was also a problem for the great majority of my patients with their husbands, wives, and lovers.

There really was only one diagnostic question I needed to answer about Charles, and that was whether he was sexually attracted to his bear *in spite* of the danger she represented or because of it. Was he the very soul of love that he claimed to be? Or was he self-destructive—a sexual masochist? This was not an academic question that I could puzzle over at my leisure. My five-week clock was already ticking.

WHEN CHARLES CAME IN the following Monday, I immediately sensed something different about his appearance, but several minutes passed before I could identify what it was: His beard was several shades lighter than it had been on Friday. He had bleached it, and I instantly knew why: Charles wanted to look more like a polar bear. I now realized that this was what his beard was about in the first place. *And* his shaggy hair. *And* his increased girth. It was all part of Charles's campaign to win Zero over. I complimented him on the job he had done on his beard.

"Looks good," I said. "Maybe it will help."

Charles smiled, obviously pleased.

I was sticking with my first instinct, to take Charles's courtship of Zero seriously. I was going to proceed as if I had two equal choices to consider: either to help Charles make his relationship with Zero more fulfilling or to help him release himself from an impossibly dangerous liaison with her. If I pressed for only the latter goal, I was certain I would lose Charles's trust. Truth to tell, deep in my "unorthodox" heart, I believe that if I had discovered there really was a way that Charles could have lived with Zero happily and safely ever after, I would have helped him seek it.

I decided to move ahead with Charles as I would have with any other case, by drawing out his personal history. I would listen, alert to clues to how he got into his "hazardous" situation in hopes of finding a clue to resolving it. I certainly did not expect to come up with some comprehensive theory that accounted for why this particular man had become eroticized by a bear. I doubted there was any such theory that I would find acceptable, just as, for example, I am skeptical of theories that purport to explain why this particular person became gay and this one did not. Such theories usually strike me as circular, ultimately citing the effect as proof of the cause.

But again I was in for a surprise.

This is the story Charles told me.

He was the sole and unexpected child of an older couple. His father, Padraic, a wealthy industrialist, was already retired by the time Charles was born, and his mother, Katherine, sickly and depressive, spent most of her time in bed. They all lived on a remote country estate where day after day would pass with barely a word exchanged, even at meals. Charles could recall only one occasion when he saw his parents touching each other. He could not remember his father ever touching him.

His father had a singular obsession: his college, Bowdoin. He felt he owed his enormous success to that institution and so was deeply involved in alumni affairs—fund raising, organizing reunions, recruiting talented applicants. His home, his clothing, even his car were replete with the Bowdoin emblem, a legacy of its most illustrious alumnus, the Arctic explorer Robert Peary, '77. That emblem was a polar bear.

"There were polar bears everywhere," Charles told me. "On the lamps, on the ashtrays, the glassware, the hooked rugs. We had Bowdoin chairs with polar bears painted on the backs in all twenty-two rooms of the house. Father had a carved polar bear pipe stand. He had polar bears painted on the sides of the station wagon that the chauffeur drove me to school in. And for my birthdays and Christmas, I always got a stuffed polar bear. I can't remember ever getting anything else. I had a good thirty of them by the time I was thirteen."

These images of the polar bear had the status of powerful totems in the Embree household: They were loved and worshiped for the gift of success that the Great Polar Bear had bestowed on Padraic. And for young Charles, these bears were more than gods; they were his sole companions. The fact is there were far more polar bears in young Charles's life than there were people, and those bears were infinitely more accessible to him than people for both intimacy and comfort.

"When I was about five, Father gave me this stuffed polar bear who was bigger than I was." Charles went on. "Her name was Lucky, and I took her with me everywhere. I had these conversations with her that would go on for hours. We'd talk about everything, absolutely everything. Lucky made jokes and gave me advice about stuff. And sometimes, when something sad happened or when we were feeling particularly lonely, we would cry together. . . . Every night I fell asleep in Lucky's arms. I loved that bear. *We loved each other.*"

I asked Charles if he spoke for Lucky during his conversations with her, but he shrugged without answering. He went on.

"When Mother gave me a bath, she called my behind Big Bear and my penis Little Bear," he said. "You know, like, 'Make sure you wash Little Bear or he'll feel left out.' "

Later in the hour he reported, "Sometimes, when Mother was feeling well enough, she liked to play this game with me where she'd put on a big fur coat—usually, she'd just put it on over her slip—and she would hunt me. She'd hide behind a door waiting for me, and when I got close, she'd suddenly pounce on me. She'd wrap her arms around me and nip at my stomach with her mouth, growling all the time."

"Like a bear," I commented.

Charles turned up his palms, as if to say, "Of course."

"And you enjoyed this game?" I asked.

"Sure. It was scary, but I loved it."

*Incredible.* Could Charles be making all of this up? It was beginning to sound almost comic, as if a Hollywood script-writer had been asked to cook up a plausible etiology of Charles's sexual obsession. I was little surprised by what Charles told me next.

"I was still sleeping with Lucky when I was twelve. She was all worn down from years of handling. Anyhow, one night when I was stroking her, I started to get excited. You know, an erection. And the next thing I knew I came all over her. A wonderful surprise. It was my first orgasm."

This soon became a regular practice.

"Lucky had an open mouth; it went in a little. So I'd rub Little Bear against Lucky until it was hard, and then I'd put Little Bear inside her mouth and come," Charles told me. "One time Mother caught me at it. She made a big fuss, but it didn't stop me from doing it again the next night."

Charles reported all of this to me in a matter-of-fact voice without any apparent embarrassment. In this last story he had reverted quite naturally to calling his penis Little Bear. And why not? It *was* perfectly natural in the context of his upbringing.

Charles saw his first live polar bear at the age of fourteen, when his father took him to the zoo for the first time.

"It was overwhelming," he told me. "I felt so excited, I couldn't stop dancing around in front of the bars. She was so big. She was alive. She moved on her own. She looked right at me. I couldn't believe it. I told my father that when I grew up, I wanted to take care of bears."

"And what did he say?"

"Oh, I'll never forget what he said," Charles told me, leaning his heavy body forward in his chair. "He said that polar bears were incredibly dangerous. But that the greatest test a man can have is to face real danger."

"And do you remember how that made you feel?"

"Yes. I was sure he was dead wrong," Charles said. "I thought you didn't need to be brave to face a bear. You just needed to be kind and loving."

It was at this point in Charles's life that both his parents began warning him about the dangers of women. They were gold diggers, his father had solemnly informed him, his mother adding that most of them had contagious, fatal diseases.

Seven years later, at the age of twenty-one, Charles had his fateful first encounter with Zero. He had gone to the circus with a college friend. There, late in the evening, Glorious Glorianna came into the center ring with three polar bears and proceeded to put them through their act of dancing, juggling, and jumping through hoops.

"I was mesmerized by Zero from the first moment I saw her," Charles told me. "I couldn't take my eyes off her. My heart started pounding. I broke into a sweat. It was like kismet or something. I fell in love with her right then and there. That night, when I got home, I couldn't get her out of my mind."

"Did you masturbate?"

"Yes."

"While thinking about her?"

"Yes."

"Did she remind you of Lucky?" I ventured.

Charles shrugged.

"I'm just wondering why Zero and not the other two bears." I pressed on.

For the first time that day Charles glared at me scornfully.

*"Why does anybody fall in love with anybody?"* he retorted, raising his voice. "There is just a connection, that's all. You know, like, 'Strangers in the Night.' "

My head was spinning. Once again Charles had brought me right to the edge of the precipice. I took a deep breath to clear my head.

"So, how did you get to know her?" I asked.

Charles eyed me critically for a moment, as if deciding whether I deserved to hear more. Finally he continued.

"I found out that in the off-season Zero and the other bears stayed in the Toledo Zoo, so Christmas break I hitchhiked out there. Glorianna was out there, too, and some afternoons she trained them in this kind of corral—brushing up the act, working out new tricks, that sort of thing."

"Well, one day I was watching them practice and one of the stools broke and a bear fell down real hard. He squealed and roared. Then he started racing around in circles, crazed. All hell broke loose. So without really thinking, I raced in to help. I'm not sure how I did it, but I calmed them all down pretty quickly. Glorianna was amazed. And she was very grateful, so grateful that she offered me a job as her assistant right on the spot. And I accepted on the spot. I never went back to NYU, didn't even pick up my things. I was exactly where I wanted to be—with the love of my life."

So ended my second session with Charles. It left me feeling even dizzier than the first.

DID I NOW HAVE a theory accounting for why Charles had become sexually fixated on a polar bear? The question is almost laughable. The truth is that if I had been asked to design a developmental model for creating a human being who would become sexually fixated on a polar bear, I could not have done a better job. In fact, considering the progression that Charles had just described to me, it was hard to imagine his having developed a primary sexual attraction to anything *other* than polar bears. Certainly not to human beings.

It was as if Padraic and Katherine Embree had deliberately covered all their bases. No brothers, sisters, or other playmates for Charles—just lifelike stuffed polar bears to talk to and play with. No loving parental contact—just bears to cuddle with. Even in her rare physical contact with Charles, Katherine had pretended to be a bear, a thrilling furry bear who nipped seductively at his naked belly. Charles was specifically taught to identify his genitalia with bears, making the sexual connection complete. And just in case Charles had any budding attraction to human women, he was informed that they were evil disease carriers.

Theories of the causes of sexual identification and deviation abound, but in this case I was perfectly happy with the simplest of them all. My authority here was not Freud or Jung, but Konrad Lorenz, the Nobel Prize winning Austrian ethologist. I remember a picture of Lorenz squatting down and waddling in front of a gaggle of newborn greylag geese whose mother had died. The geese, genetically predisposed to follow the first "waddler" they encountered, immediately formed a line behind Lorenz and waddled after him, instantly bonding with him. Thenceforth they behaved toward Lorenz as they would have toward a mother goose. This, the animal behaviorist wrote, was an example of that quintessential interplay of nature and nurture known as imprinting.

It seemed clear to me that Charles had simply "sexually imprinted" on polar bears. The natural unfocused sexual drive he had been born with attached itself to the one thing that was comforting, "personal," sensual, stimulating, and specifically genital in his young world. A polar bear was the primary object that his awakening sexuality had looked upon, and thus he pursued it with the soul of love.

But what did this tell me about Charles's relation to self-destructive impulses? Certainly his mother's "stalking bear" game had been deliciously scary. And his father had taught him that the true test of his manhood would be in overcoming a dangerous bear. Did these elements suggest that his attraction to Zero was rooted in masochism?

I did not think so. My sense was that elements of danger and power were at best secondary to the intimacy and sensuality inherent to Charles's basic sexual imprinting. I now believed more than ever that Charles had fallen in love with Zero quite as naturally as I had fallen in love with my wife.

I remember feeling excited and elated that Monday afternoon. Perhaps the clock was ticking, but I was much farther ahead of the game than I had ever expected to be after only two sessions with Charles. Yet where did I go from here, convinced as I was that the nature of Charles's "deviant" desires was virtually inevitable? In a sense my job might have been easier if Charles *had* been a masochist; at least then the "danger" would have been inseparable from the "disease." But such was not the case. I had no stake in making Charles "normal," just in keeping him alive. How was I to go about getting him to decathect from his natural love object? This appeared no easier than trying to "cure" a homosexual.

THINGS DID NOT GO WELL in the following weeks.

Charles struck me as so conscious and rational that I thought I could try dead-on logic with him. Yes, you love Zero, I argued, but there is no way you can ever get her to love you. Surely, you see that? But Charles argued back bitterly that I had no faith in the power of love. It would ultimately prevail over Zero's resistance.

On the surface this sounds like a pathological delusion, but in fact, Charles's response was no different from most of my other patients who were stubbornly stuck in impossible relationships. It will work out, they would insist. It just needs time. Love is never easy, but it conquers all.

Another week passed, and Charles was getting plumper with every visit. His hair and beard were now bleached completely white. I again complimented him on his bearlike appearance. I was getting absolutely nowhere.

Then I came up with what I thought was an ingenious approach. Look, I suggested in reasonable tones, Zero most certainly loves you, too, but she cannot control her dangerous beastly impulses no matter how much she would like to. So you have to help her control them, and this will necessarily entail extreme measures. Why don't you subdue her with an injection of tranquilizers whenever you want to be intimate with her?

As I expected, Charles found this idea extremely repugnant. It was disrespectful of Zero; it amounted to nothing less than premeditated rape. Charles became furious with me because my approach "dehumanized" Zero. But she wasn't human; that was my point. Couldn't Charles see that his novel situation required novel rules of conduct? How, indeed, did he intend to make Zero "safe"? If not this extreme measure, then what?

But Charles would not budge beyond his fury at my "insulting" suggestion, and he remained angry at me for the next

four sessions. Three weeks had passed, and I was running out
of ideas.

On Monday of the fourth week Charles did not show up for
his scheduled hour. Nor did he that Friday or the following
Monday. I became so concerned about him that I would sometimes find myself worrying about him while I was working
with other patients—a cardinal sin in my profession. On Monday I finally called the circus in New Jersey. The woman who
took my call was surprisingly circumspect. She would tell me
nothing about Charles, just that she would take a message
for him.

On Friday Charles came into my office at his appointed
hour with a wide white bandage circling his neck and his right
arm in a sling. He let himself down in his chair gingerly,
flinching from pain. I did not ask him what had happened. I
did not need to.

"I thought we had a deal," I said after a long silence.

Charles shrugged. "We weren't getting anywhere anyhow,"
he replied, not looking at me.

"We still have time."

"We're virtually finished," Charles said.

"*You* are virtually finished," I retorted sharply. "Look at
you!"

Charles did not say a word for several minutes. He kept
shifting in his chair, as if about to rise and leave, but he remained seated. I waited.

"I'll tell you something, Doctor," he said, finally. "Coming
in here and talking about Zero all the time just makes me want
her all the more. Sure, now I know why I fell in love with a
bear—that wasn't hard to figure out—but it doesn't change a
thing. Does knowing why ever change anything?"

"Sometimes," I answered.

"Well, let me tell you something else," Charles said bitterly.

"I'm not taking any more insults from you about her. That's not what I came here for."

"What *did* you come here for, Charles?"

Charles shrugged. "I don't even know anymore," he said dismally.

I now suspected that I had done absolutely everything wrong with Charles. By initially accepting his love of Zero as "normal," by demonstrating that it was a "natural" outcome of his upbringing, I had given Charles corroboration of his passionate impulse. In a sense I had given his love the one thing it was missing: "parental" approval. Then, by turning around and hammering away at Zero's dangerous "bestial" nature, I had pushed Charles into the position of defending her, of "standing up for the one he loved." He certainly did sound as though he were more attached to her now than when he had come in four weeks ago.

I looked over at Charles. With his neck swathed in white bandages and his bushy beard whiter than ever, he did indeed look wild and woolly, half man, half beast. At that moment he looked to me as if he really did belong in a cage.

It was not too late for that. I could suggest that now, and if Charles refused to commit himself to a mental hospital—and I was pretty sure he would refuse—I probably could convince his parents that it was in Charles's best interest that *they* commit him. I would tell them that he needed to be incarcerated as a form of "protective custody." There was not a doubt in my mind that one more nocturnal trip into Zero's cage would finish Charles off for good. I no longer cared if his incarceration amounted to an admission of my own failure. I would not be able to live with myself if a lapse in my professional judgment were to contribute to Charles's death.

I was literally within seconds of putting this plan into action when a remarkable idea popped into my head—remarkable yet, in retrospect, totally obvious.

"You know, Charles, neither of us has really been fair to Zero in here," I said. "I mean, you're always talking about how you feel about Zero, and I'm always talking about how I feel about your relationship to Zero. But she's always left out of it."

Charles eyed me warily. "What are you talking about now, Doctor?"

"I'm talking about respect," I said. "I'm talking about there always being two sides to every relationship, and I've been hearing only one."

Charles looked apprehensive. I took that as a good sign.

"You see, I think you are right, Charles: You and I have done just about all we can do together at this point." I went on. "So let me tell you what I usually do with couples who are having problems like yours: I see them together. So I can hear both sides. Couple therapy."

Charles's jaw had sagged. I did not want to give him a chance to argue with me, so I immediately stood up, walked over to my closet, and withdrew my jacket.

"Let's go," I said.

Charles remained seated.

"I—I don't really see—" he stammered.

"What have we got to lose?" I interjected, opening my office door. I knew *I* had nothing to lose; this was my last chance.

Charles hesitated a moment longer, then lifted himself heavily out of his chair and followed me out the door. While we waited for the elevator, I stuck my head inside my apartment and asked my wife to cancel my appointments for the rest of the day. She saw Charles lingering behind me and did not ask me why.

CHARLES DROVE US TO New Jersey in his car, a Volkswagen "beetle" that barely accommodated his hefty torso behind the wheel. I offered to drive, considering that Charles's injury left him with only one arm to steer, but he declined, saying that he felt uneasy when other people drove. He immediately switched on the radio to an "easy listening" station. I was happy not to have to talk.

As we crossed the George Washington Bridge, I rolled open my window and let the river air blow against my face. I felt giddy and frightened at the same time, not unlike a little boy running away to the circus. I did not want to rehearse in my mind for whatever was coming up; I don't think I would have known how to if I had tried.

The circus was set up on fairgrounds not far from the Palisades. Although it was late in the morning when we arrived, most of the people there appeared to have just gotten out of bed. Sitting outside their trailers on plastic lawn chairs, they nodded to Charles and me over mugs of coffee. I wondered if they knew the exact circumstances of Charles's injuries. If they did, they probably thought little of it. Circus people, I imagined, were not easily shocked.

Charles silently led me past the closed concession stands, their red and gold trim glinting in the late-morning sun, to the rear of the big top. There, on the far side of a parking lot, was the animal area. As we approached, I could see the heads of several elephants parading inside their pen. One of them looked directly at me with a single beady black eye as we walked by, then raised his trunk and gave a short toot. Horses were next, then lions. The final three cages were somewhat removed from the others; each contained a single polar bear.

I was not prepared for their sheer size. The first bear, a male, was standing at the front of his cage as we approached. He was easily nine feet tall and weighed a good thousand pounds.

"Good morning, Bendix," Charles said to the bear, almost as if he were greeting an office mate.

Bendix did not respond.

The second bear appeared smaller, but it was hard to tell as he was lying down, asleep. Zero was in the last cage in the row. She was sitting upright, her legs bowed in front with her heels together, her arms resting easily in her lap. In this position she looked remarkably benign, almost like an over-sized teddy bear. She was considerably smaller than either of the males, only about six hundred pounds.

She immediately turned her head toward Charles as we came into view. Charles smiled, nodding gently, but said nothing. For a couple of seconds they silently regarded each other. I would not presume to guess what was going on in that bear's mind or heart, but what I saw went beyond mere recognition, even beyond the acknowledgment of long-standing comfortable familiarity that, say, transpires between my horse and myself when I approach her. What I saw passing between Charles and Zero looked remarkably like human intimacy.

At that moment I tried with all of my imagination to empathize with Charles, to feel what it would be like to love this bear as a man loves a woman. To lust after her. I confess that I could not do that. I could not even get a sense of what it would be like. I can pop myself into the leading role in many a strange fantasy, but this was not one of them.

Now Zero saw me and rose on all fours, emitting a soft growl. She clearly was not pleased with my presence. I quickly surveyed the area. There was no one else in sight. I turned to Charles.

"Okay, let's get started," I said.

Charles folded his arms across his chest. I could see a sneer of resentment forming on his lips.

"You came all the way out here to make a fool of me, didn't you?" he said, spitting out the words.

"No, that's not true," I replied softly.

"Well, this is ridiculous, and you know it." Charles continued bitterly. "You don't understand Zero. You can't possibly understand her."

"I know that," I said. "But *you* understand her. I can see that very clearly."

"And what's that supposed to mean?" he said challengingly.

"It means that you can help her out," I said. "Help her express what she feels. Give her a voice."

My heart was pounding. I was flying by the seat of my pants, improvising as I went along.

"What are you talking about now, Akeret?"

"I have some questions for Zero," I said. "Some things that might be helpful to know. I wondered if you could help her answer them."

Charles stared back at me. I noticed that under his beard his cheeks were reddening. He did not protest. I jumped in.

"What I would like to know," I said quietly, "is what it feels like being locked up in there?"

"I hate it!" Charles shot back. He looked surprised at the vehemence of the words that came out of his mouth.

"Why's that?"

"Why? Because it drives me crazy, that's why. Stir crazy. I can barely turn around in here. And I don't have a shred of privacy. It's degrading!"

I did not have time to wonder how or why Charles had entered so completely into his role as Zero. It was incredible. It was wonderful. I pressed on.

"You must be angry then," I said.

"You bet I am!"

"Who are you angry at?"

Charles took a deep breath. He hunched his shoulders, then shot his right hand forward, as if pawing the air.

"Glorianna," he replied. "Most of all, Glorianna and her goddamned whip. But the others, too. Jack and Tulio."

"And Charles?" I said.

Charles hesitated. He slowly turned back to the cage and looked at Zero. She had come up to the bars and was standing on her hind legs, looking out at us.

"No, not Charles," Charles replied softly. "Charles cares for me."

"Is that so?" I said. I was operating on sheer instinct. "Then why don't you ask Charles to let you out of there? If he loves you, he should be willing to do that for you."

Charles's face flushed, and I could see beads of sweat forming on his forehead. He turned back toward the cage, his hands fumbling in his pocket. I heard a jingling sound.

My heart jumped. Keys! That was the sound of the keys to Zero's cage. I had played this too far, way too far, and now I was going to pay for it. My personal high wire act had failed; my bluff had been called. I would have to stop Charles from opening the cage, of course. And then I would have no choice but to end this charade and commit him to a mental institution, as I undoubtedly should have done in the first place.

Suddenly Charles turned back to me. He was trembling, and there were tears in his eyes.

"I don't like this game, Akeret," he said. "It stinks. You're a cruel man. Very cruel."

I stared back at him.

"I could kill you, Charles," I said.

*"What?"*

"*I* am speaking for Zero now," I said. I let this sink in and then repeated, "I could kill you, Charles."

Charles turned slowly back to the cage. He was looking directly into Zero's eyes.

"Maybe you should," he whispered. "Maybe you should kill me, Zero. God knows, I've failed you over and over again."

He loved her. He really did. And that, of course, was all I had to work with.

"Sometimes I really would like to kill you," I said. "But if I did, they would kill me. Put me down immediately. They always do that when an animal kills a human, no matter whose fault it really is. They have to."

Charles's chest was heaving. I could see that tears were slipping down his cheeks now.

"I—I'm sorry, Zero," he stammered.

"Leave me alone, Charles," I said softly, tenderly. "Leave me in peace. Please, please, just leave me."

Charles was sobbing. Several minutes passed before he spoke.

"All right, Zero," he whispered. "I'll leave you in peace."

Charles turned slowly back to me, still crying hard. I walked up and hugged him, like a father embracing a long-neglected son.

I stayed with Charles for the rest of that day while he packed up his things and made his good-byes, then helped him move into a friend's apartment in Manhattan that afternoon. In my judgment, our work had just begun that day, and I was eager to see where we would go with it next. Perhaps I had saved his life, but only for now. In the long run I hoped to help him live not only a longer life but a more fulfilling one.

Charles said he would see me the next day at his scheduled hour, but he did not show up. Nor did he show up the next day or the next. I tried calling him, but to no avail. Two weeks later a letter arrived from him posted in London. It contained a postal order for sixty dollars, his outstanding bill. His note read: "I wish I could say that I was happy, but I can only say that I am alive. Yet for that you have my undying gratitude. Charles."

THE HALLWAY outside Charles's Sarasota apartment was strewn with open cartons containing books, folders, newspaper clippings, and photographs. I hesitated in front of his door. Over the past thirty years I had often been visited by terrifying images of Charles's creeping back into Zero's cage for one final fatal assignation. When I located Charles in Florida and discovered that he was alive and well and holding joint appointments at the theater department of the University of Florida and at Clown College, I felt a terrific burden lift off me. That, I thought as I stood at Charles's door, was as much satisfaction as I could ask for. Just as had happened with Isabella, I was seized by the urge to turn around and leave well enough alone.

I didn't, of course.

Charles opened after a single knock, grabbed my outstretched hand, and shook it hard.

"My savior!" He laughed.

He was heavier than when I saw him last and was completely bald on top with a short white fringe of hair on the sides and a neatly trimmed white beard. Obviously he no longer needed bleach for this effect. He wore metal-rimmed glasses that gave him a decidedly Kriss Kringle appearance. He looked cheerful and surprisingly old. He removed a pile of circus posters from an upholstered chair and gestured for me to sit down.

"One of these years I'm going to clean this place up," he said with a smile. "Not that anybody ever comes up here."

The hallway had only been a preview of Charles's interior decorating style. His entire duplex apartment was overflowing with books, papers, and various models and artifacts of circus life, including scores of juggler's balls and clubs. The decor may have been typical of an eccentric professor's retreat, but I could not help seeing it as an animal's lair.

Before he said another word, Charles rubbed the sleeve of his shirt over the cover of a book and handed it to me. It was a text on the history and art of juggling. The authors were Charles Embree and Yvonne Armato.

"It's in its ninth edition," he said proudly.

"Fabulous!" I replied, much impressed. "You've certainly made a life of it, haven't you? The circus, I mean."

"It's my whole life," Charles replied, clearing a spot on the sofa so he could sit down across from me.

"So, who was your coauthor, this, uh, Yvonne Armato?" I asked, consulting the cover again.

Charles's face flushed. "You always did have a nose for the nub of things," he said.

I nodded.

"It's a long story," Charles said, looking a bit uncomfortable.

"I like long stories."

"Yes, I remember that, too," Charles said. He took a couple of slow, deep breaths, like an acrobat preparing for a dangerous jump.

"I've been thinking about your visit ever since you called me up out of the blue," he said. "What I was going to tell you and what I wasn't. Rehearsing. That's something I always tell my juggling students: Performance is easy; rehearsal is hard."

I smiled.

"Anyhow, I decided that one thing I wasn't going to talk about was Yvonne," he said.

"That's certainly your privilege," I said.

Charles abruptly laughed. "But I've suddenly changed my mind," he said. "I always tell my students that the best performances are pure improvisation."

I laughed with him.

"But let's start first with day one, uh?" he said. "I suppose you know that little trip we took out to New Jersey a couple hundred years ago sort of gave me a new perspective on my life. An epiphany you'd probably call it. Although I've always wondered if you really had any idea what was going on in my mind that day."

He eyed me critically over the tops of his glasses.

"Probably not," I said. "But for the record, I thought that you got a very hard look at what could happen if you didn't change."

"You believed I was operating out of love, didn't you?" he said, an edge to his voice.

"Yes, I do," I replied.

"Well, I'm afraid you were wrong," he said triumphantly. "The only love I felt that day was for myself. Self-love. My little epiphany was nothing more than the remarkable realization that living was better than dying. That there was more of a future in it."

I smiled. I did not entirely believe that was all there was to Charles's change of heart that long-past day in front of Zero's cage, but I could very well understand his need to deny a more selfless motive. I still believed that his basic decision had been to sacrifice his love for his beloved's sake, but I also knew that would have been a terrible decision to live with for the rest of his life; a selfish change of heart is less susceptible to the pain of regret.

"So, where did you disappear to after that?" I asked.

"I trekked all over Europe for months," he said. "I took in every circus I could find, from Copenhagen to Sardinia. It was the first time I ever saw small, one-ring circuses, and they were a wonder to behold. Artistic, not glitzy. Intimate. Full of real drama, not just effects. I fell in love with the circus all over again.

"It was during that year that I really perfected my juggling. Took it to the streets in Amsterdam and Paris. Paris was full of street entertainers then. There was a guy in front of Les Deux Magots who had this needle and razor blade act. He stuck needles through his lips and razor blades under his eyelids. My act was sort of refreshing after that. I juggled cups and saucers. . . . I lived on the cheap. Youth hostels. Sometimes I even slept in the park. The world was a safer place back then.

"When I came back to New York, I landed two jobs right off the bat. Two perfect jobs. One was cataloging masks in Low Library up at Columbia University. They have this incredible mask collection. And my other job was at this club Andy Warhol had just started downtown, The Electric Circus. I juggled and did a little mime I'd picked up in Europe. This was the sixties, and the clubs were all strobe lights. Let me tell you, just about anybody can look good doing mime under strobe lights."

Charles chuckled.

"Tell me about those masks," I said.

"Ah, ever the shrink, eh, Akeret?" Charles said, the edge back in his voice again. "A fascination with masks means you are looking for a way to hide, right? Disguising yourself from the world?"

This was the second time Charles had challenged me since I'd arrived. I wondered what it was about.

"That's one theory, yes," I answered.

"Well, here's another theory, Akeret," Charles said. "And it's just the opposite of yours. I think wearing masks is a way of showing who you really are. Like there's a clown in everybody just aching to get out, but we hold it in with our furrowed brows and stiff upper lips. Those brows and lips—*they* are the real masks. But paint on a clown face and the real you sees daylight. Those commedia dell'arte masks that I cataloged—they were mirrors of the soul, not disguises."

I found Charles's theory compelling, but I still had to wonder at the degree of his defensiveness.

"All right, now we come to Yvonne." Charles said after a moment. "She was a student of mine at Fordham. That was my first teaching job, probably the first position teaching circus arts at any major university. Yvonne was a drama major who wanted to be a juggler, and she was a natural. Great balance, great reflexes. Quick learner. I immediately put her in my act at The Electric Circus. We passed seven clubs at a time. Big hit.

"She was my student for four years, and then I married her. It seemed like the natural thing to do. We had big plans. We created our own commedia company in the Venice style—stilt walking, masks, mime, juggling. We gave performances in a loft down in the Bowery and sometimes in Central Park. Those were fabulous years, the best circusing I've ever done."

Charles sighed a deep and troubled sigh. The Yvonne story was not going to end well, that was for sure.

"We wrote the juggling book together just a couple years after we were married. Yvonne did the photographs. That was in '72. That means it's been in print for over twenty years, right? Well, a couple of years ago I told the publisher to change Yvonne's last name on the new edition. Make it her maiden name again."

"How long were you married?"

"Ten, almost eleven years." Charles gave me a hard look. "She left *me*, if that's what you're wondering. Ran off with a handsome young man, an actor. She broke my heart. Completely and utterly broke my heart. Smashed it right in two."

Charles's Kriss Kringle twinkle had completely vanished.

"The hazards of love, eh, Akeret?" he said caustically.

That line echoed across thirty years. I was once again reminded that a fourteen-stitch claw cut was nothing as compared with a broken heart. One question after another surged in my mind: Had he loved Yvonne the same way that he had loved Zero? How had the sex gone with Yvonne? What was the transition from bear to woman like? Had he ever completely gotten over Zero?

But Charles had started talking again, and now the source of that edge in his voice was becoming clear: It was bitterness.

"You never know who's going to get it in the end, do you, Akeret? It's a damned conceit to think that you do. Did you ever hear what happened to Glorious Glorianna?"

"No."

"Dead," Charles said. "Stomped on the head by one of her elephants. During solo practice. Topaz was his name—the elephant's name. They couldn't get into the cage for almost an hour. Topaz was guarding the body. He had to be destroyed, of course. Topaz. That was less than two years after I'd left."

I shook my head sympathetically.

"Hey, it's no big deal in the circus, Akeret. They say one elephant keeper a year gets crunched."

Charles's face was animated again. He had clearly enjoyed telling me this story. I was beginning to feel a bit uncomfortable.

"Or how about Dr. Goldman? Remember Goldman?" Charles went on, leaning forward on the sofa.

"What about him?" I had lost contact with Goldman some twenty years ago.

"I guess you didn't hear then. They cut the counseling program at NYU, so he got a job counseling parolees for the Department of Corrections. But that didn't last long. You know why? Because they found him beaten to death in his bathtub. One of his parolees didn't like his brand of therapy." Charles looked me straight in the eye and smiled. "Another hazardous line of work, uh?"

A shiver passed across my shoulders. Charles's point was abundantly clear: One takes risks whatever one does, so who is to judge what is safe to try and what is not? What is worth a risk and what is not? And of course, by implication, who was I to have made that judgment for him? That, undoubtedly, was what this bitterness was about.

But some risks are greater than others, I thought. Like trying to make love to a polar bear, for example. I didn't say this, of course. I knew I had to be careful. Charles's taste for the macabre was new to me, and it was disturbing, even a bit frightening. The thought occurred to me that I might be at risk myself, that perhaps the safest thing for me to do would be to get out of here right now.

"Anyhow, it took me ten years to get over Yvonne." Charles suddenly went on, his voice vulnerable-sounding again. "God

knows, I tried to win her back. I asked her what had gone
wrong, and she just said that there wasn't enough feeling there
for her. Not enough *passion*. I guess she found that with this
other guy. The sex, the passion."

This was the opening I'd been waiting for, but I hesitated,
not sure how wise it was to press on. My curiosity won out.

"And was the passion there for *you*, Charles?"

Charles lowered his eyes. For a long moment he was silent.

"You mean, like it was with Zero?" he said.

"Yes, like with Zero."

Charles took a deep breath and let it out slowly. "She's
dead, too, you know," he said. "Died young. Caught the flu
and died."

"I'm sorry to hear that."

Charles was again silent.

"So, you want to know about me and passion, uh?" he said
at last. "Well, there's not a whole lot to say. Remember that
movie *A Clockwork Orange?* Remember at the end when they
conditioned that boy to cut off his feelings the moment he felt
them? Well, that's me. If you flashed a picture of a polar bear,
I'd respond, all right. I'd get excited, but then right away I'd
get cut off. That was my cure. Instant cutoff from all passion.
. . . Hey, it saved my life, right, Akeret?"

I did not answer. I just sat there, stunned. For thirty years
I had worried that my therapy with Charles had failed in the
worst possible way—that overcome with passion, he had
searched out Zero and sneaked back into her cage for a final,
fatal encounter. That was not hard to imagine. After all, how
long did I expect the effects of a few minutes of therapy in front
of a bear cage to last? Improvised therapy at that?

But what Charles was telling me was that our therapy had
worked beyond my wildest expectations. It was as if I had
subjected him to the most extreme form of aversion condition-
ing, complete with electric shocks. And it had worked so well
that *all* of Charles's sexual passion had been cut off. To save his

life, I had amputated his soul—his soul of love. I very much doubted that this was the whole story; it could not possibly be as simple as that. But I was sure that was the way Charles saw it. Little wonder he felt so bitter toward me.

Yet now I saw that Charles was looking at me with a warm smile, a smile that seemed to promise the possibility of forgiveness.

"I'll tell you one thing, Akeret," he said. "We were ahead of our time. Way ahead. Do you know how many friends I've lost to AIDS in the last five years? Try twenty-four. Twenty-four men who died before they were fifty just because they wanted to make love. Because they couldn't help themselves."

"Do you really think they knew the risk they were taking?"

"I bet a lot of them did, sure. They started out trying to lead a safe life, but then in the heat of a moment they said the hell with it and did something crazy. You know, like the moth and the flame. At the moment it seems worth it to risk your life. To feel so passionately alive for an hour or two that you are willing to die for it."

"And is it worth it?" I asked.

Charles laughed. "That's the sixty-four-thousand-dollar question, isn't it?"

"Yes, it is."

Charles shook his head back and forth a few times, then abruptly laughed again. "Are you as hungry as I am?" he asked.

"I sure am."

"You buying, Doctor?"

"You bet."

CHARLES TOOK US TO a café called The High Wire, up near Venice. The walls were covered with photographs of circus people and circus acts going back a hundred years. Prominent among them was an enlarged photograph of the famous midget Tom Thumb, standing on the flexed biceps of a strong man. It was midafternoon, but the place was packed, and Charles seemed to know everyone there. After I had spent the morning with him in his solitary, claustrophobic apartment, it was a pleasure to see him out among people with whom he seemed so comfortable.

Over lunch Charles filled me in on his professional life. He taught not only juggling and performance techniques in the drama department of the university but also a course on the history of the circus from Roman times to the present. He was currently developing a course—and possibly a book—on the circus in film. I asked him what his favorite circus movie was.

*"Freaks,"* he replied immediately, referring to an American classic about a circus midget who falls hopelessly in love with a beautiful and cruel trapeze artist.

"Mine, too," I said.

Charles told me about his extensive travels in Egypt, collecting ancient juggling artifacts and lore. One of his discoveries was the Egyptian goddess named Isis who is pictured on vases and baskets juggling a clublike object with two other women.

"It turns out they're juggling the penis of this guy Osiris," he said. "And one day, so a version of the story goes, they missed, the penis went flying into the river, and a fish gulped it down."

Charles laughed.

"I've always felt a kind of mystical kinship with old Osiris," he said.

It was only a few minutes later that two tall, leather-clad young women—one blond, the other a redhead—approached our table. Charles introduced them as Rikki and Gretchen.

"Are you circus performers, too?" I asked.

"Why, of course," Rikki replied rather haughtily. "We work with Charles. Didn't he tell you?"

Charles's face flushed. Gretchen gave his beard a playful yank, and the two women moved on to friends at another table. Charles lowered his eyes. I busied myself with my salad.

"Look, I'm just wired differently from other people," Charles said quietly, not looking up. "Always have been."

"And I don't judge people," I replied. "Never did."

Without thinking why, I reached my hand across the table. Charles took it, and we shook warmly. A few minutes later he jotted a downtown Sarasota address on a napkin and handed it to me.

"It's called the Pyramid Club," he said. "Our act goes on at around midnight."

I said that I would be there.

BACK AT MY MOTEL I took a vigorous twenty-minute swim, then retired to my room and fell immediately into a dreamless sleep. When I awoke, the sun was already down. Not knowing what to expect, I dressed in blazer and tie. I ate in the motel coffee shop. At eleven I set off for the Pyramid Club.

It turned out to be in the bohemian quarter, a section of town that I'd missed on my earlier explorations. It was lined with galleries and cafés and esoteric shops. One of the latter was called Alter Image, and at first glance, I thought it was simply a women's sexy apparel shop, but a closer look in its window revealed that the women's clothes were tailored to fit men's bodies. The Pyramid Club was next door.

I would not be telling the truth if I claimed that I felt perfectly at ease inside the Pyramid Club. For starters, I was overdressed, if that is the right word. Much of the clientele, men *and* women, wore tight-fighting leather pants and open leather vests over bare torsos. I was also easily the oldest person there, a good thirty years above the average age. Some of the couples were obviously gay; others I was not so sure of, in part because the cross-dressers among them were so artful.

Rather than take a table, I sat at the bar and ordered a glass of white wine. The music was loud and strident; the dancers on the narrow space in front of the stage were athletic and introspective; although they danced in couples, they all seemed to be doing solos. I looked at my watch: five to twelve.

Moments later the music stopped. A muscular young man in lederhosen rolled out a drum set, sat down, and beat a fanfare. Then another young man, wearing tails but no shirt, stepped to the microphone.

"The best things in life go around in circles," he said sardonically. "That is why we all love the circus so." And then, after another drumroll, he introduced the first act, "Gretchen, Rikki, and *the Professor!*"

Charles came out alone, dressed as Pierrot in white tights, three-cornered hat, and mask. He took a deep bow to scattered applause. The march from Prokofiev's *Love for Three Oranges* issued over the sound system. Charles produced three oranges and proceeded to juggle them, then added another and another until there were seven in all. He was very good, casually adept and quite funny; he would act as though he'd completely forgotten one of the airborne oranges until it was almost too late, then dive and catch it just before it hit the ground. The audience seemed unimpressed, restless.

Then Rikki, the tall blond woman I had met that afternoon at The High Wire, stepped out onto the stage. In opera hat, red tails, and knee-high boots over fishnet stockings, she reminded me of Marlene Dietrich in *The Blue Angel*. All she wore under her jacket was a lace half bra, bikini panties, and a garter belt. In her right hand was a black, long-handled whip. Rikki was the circus ringmaster / mistress, and she found her juggler wanting.

"Higher!" she demanded of Charles. "Can't you get it up any higher?"

Laughter rippled through the audience. They were watching the show attentively now. Charles looked beseechingly at Rikki and trembled, then tossed the oranges higher. I felt a knot twisting in the pit of my stomach.

A high-flying orange sailed out of Charles's reach and landed with a splat at the ringmistress's feet. She immediately lashed out at Charles, the long whip wrapping around his torso, the tip snapping sharply against his chest. Even from where I was standing at the bar, I could see Charles wince, his eyes smart. Suddenly all the oranges were falling to the floor. Rikki snapped the whip at Charles again and again. The audience was spellbound.

The knot in my stomach had risen to my throat. I swallowed hard, trying to hold it down. I wanted to turn away, but I forced myself to keep watching as now Gretchen paraded out onto the stage and joined them. Gretchen peeled off her black stockings and proceeded to bind Charles's hands and feet with them. Both women began whipping him hard, as the music blared on. I felt nauseated. I was utterly revolted by the spectacle of this aging, white-bearded man being beaten—this misbegotten, frail-hearted boy I had once tried so desperately to save from his own tragic impulses.

*Disgust . . . revulsion . . . nausea.* Was this the reaction of a man who did not judge? Of a therapist who had prided himself throughout his long career on always being suspect of "official" concepts of normal behavior? When it came down to cases, was I a prude in liberal's clothing? Did I find some "perversions" acceptable, while I found others disgusting? Forget about the paraphiliacs with innocent victims, the pederasts and rapists; their acts, of course, are unacceptable. But what of this willing whipping boy? Why was this behavior revolting, while, say, loving a polar bear was not? Was it simply a matter of my own personal taste? Was I soft on polar bears?

"He is so bad!" Gretchen was screeching.

"We should teach *him* how to juggle," Rikki cried, aiming her whip at Charles's groin. "Show him what *we'd* do with a pair of balls!"

The audience howled.

I dropped my money on the bar and walked out of the Pyramid Club into the warm night air. I had finally understood where my revulsion was coming from. It was not simply the brutality of the whipping that offended me. It was something deeper and more personal than that. I knew Charles; I knew his true desires. And this sadomasochistic farce I had just witnessed was a *perversion* in the basic sense of that word: It was a *misdirection of desires.* Not of statistically "normal" desires but of *Charles's original and true desires.*

With my help Charles had forsaken his most passionate desire—and its object—a long time ago. God knows, he had attempted to modify his nature, to adapt it to loving Yvonne, a woman with whom he apparently had so much in common. But without genuine sexual desire for her, that relationship had failed.

Still, Charles wanted to feel *something,* so he had turned to this perverse circus game in an attempt to get his passion back. "Where poetry fails, brutality doth succeed." And in the grand scheme of things, playing whipping boy to a pair of dominatrices was more socially acceptable—and far safer—than attempting to make love to a polar bear. After all, there were clubs like the Pyramid in cities all over the world, but I doubt that there was a single one for polar bear lovers.

And so ultimately these S-M games were a substitute for the feeling Charles could not permit himself: his "bestial" love of Zero. Ironically, that original feeling *was* romantic, *was* poetic, while this substitute with human beings was a crude and spurious love. I still did not believe that Charles's attraction to Zero was masochistic, that its potential for punishment was what excited him. Yet Charles's pure love for the bear had perforce been perverted and in the process something truly bestial had been born in him.

That, above all, was what pained me. I mourned the loss of pure love, of poetry in Charles's heart.

I SLEPT POORLY most of that night, then fell into a deep sleep near morning. When I awoke, the red light on my telephone was flashing. Charles had called, the desk clerk told me. He wanted me to meet him in the big top down in Venice at noon. I had less than an hour to dress and get there.

One section of the bleachers was almost completely filled with young people when I arrived. With their scrubbed, eager faces, their sweat shirts, jeans, and sneakers, they might have been students at any university. Their sweat shirts declared their alma mater was Clown College. I took a seat on the side, not far from where I'd watched the beautiful aerialist rehearse two days before.

Charles was standing just inside the center ring. He was wearing dark slacks and an open Oxford shirt. He nodded to me as I sat down, then continued with his lecture. He was comparing circus acts with other types of dramas—with Shakespearean comedies and French bedroom farces, with Pirandello and Beckett. It was a wonderfully entertaining lecture. Charles would quote a passage from a play, then do a piece of mime or a round of juggling that somehow paralleled the quoted scene. The students clearly loved it, and so did I.

I must remember this, I told myself. I knew that I would never be able to shake off completely the grotesque images of Charles from the night before, but I must remember this, too. For if ever a man transformed his beastly drives into something beautiful and intelligent and inspiring, it was Charles. He was among only a couple dozen American men and women who had brought circus arts into the universities, who had heralded the renaissance of the intimate, magical circus on this side of the Atlantic. It was a fine achievement, and it was, in a very true sense, the product of a personal passion, of love. This, too, is part of the picture of what became of Charles Embree.

When the class was over and the students had left, I went up to Charles. I told him how much I had enjoyed his lecture, how impressed I was with his work.

"You left early last night," he said, looking me straight in the eye.

"Yes, I did," I replied. I hesitated a moment and then added, "It's just a personal thing, but I liked today's performance much better than that one."

Charles smiled warmly at me. "Me, too," he said.

A few minutes later we shook hands again, and I walked back to my van.

Driving off, I found myself smiling. It had suddenly occurred to me that maybe Charles's performance at the Pyramid Club had been inspired by true love after all. Maybe as he entertained the audience under Rikki's cracking whip, Charles was totally identifying with his beloved Zero, the performing bear. Perhaps this was his ultimate tribute of love.

# THREE

# Seth: The Real Thing

Formal texts, journal articles, and lectures portray therapy as precise and systematic, with carefully delineated stages, strategic technical interventions, the methodical development and resolution of transference, analysis of object relations, and a careful, rational program of insight-offering interpretations. Yet I believe deeply that when no one is looking, the therapist throws in the "real thing."

Irvin D. Yalom, *Existential Psychotherapy*

ABOUT THREE YEARS AGO I fell into a terrible depression. God knows, I had been through down cycles before. Few people who have risked anything at all in their lives manage to make it to their sixties without at least a few brief periods of genuine depression—a loss of faith and confidence, feelings of meaninglessness, a major depletion of energy.

But what hit me in early 1991 was an entirely different animal. It could be argued that it only differed from other depressions in degree, but this particular degree was so great that it felt like nothing I had ever known before. It felt as if Death had invaded my mind and heart and I were powerless to resist it.

What set all this in motion was the basest of ambitions: greed. A friend had given me a "hot tip" on a stock that was sure to double in value in a month's time, two months at the most. The details of why I believed him and why I put my entire savings into this "sure thing" are not worth repeating; what greed does not account for, naïveté does. My tipster was right about the two months; that's all it took for me to lose every penny I had. There were several people dependent on me at that time: my wife; my two youngest children, who were still in college and graduate school; my ninety-year-old mother in Switzerland. I had let them all down.

There was certainly much for me to feel wretched about, to feel desperate and guilty about. Much to panic about, too. Stronger men than I would lose their bearings under the same circumstances. But I lost more than my bearings. I lost my grip.

I could not sleep. There was a throbbing emptiness that radiated from the pit of my stomach up to my chest and down into my groin. I felt numb, weak, dry. My tongue was perpetually coated with a fuzz that looked like white mold. My heartbeat hurt.

I could not tolerate the sound of the human voice. It cut into me like acid poured through a funnel into my ear. In spite of this, I tried to keep seeing my patients, not so much for the income as because I did not want to let them down—not them, too. But ultimately that proved impossible. One morning I asked my daughter Julie to phone my patients for me, to cancel all appointments indefinitely.

I ranted. For example, the sight and smell of dog feces on the streets of my neighborhood sent me into a screaming rage.

I cried, sometimes for hours at a time, until it felt as if I were vomiting with nothing left inside.

I could not think straight for more than a couple of minutes. I had no appetite for food or sex. Nothing, not even my beautiful little grandson, Will, brought me pleasure.

I sought the help of a psychopharmacologist, who immediately put me on a medication that made me feel even crazier.

I tried to talk to him about what had happened, what was happening. I could not begin to name it. I could barely talk. He tried another medication. Nothing. Another. Still nothing.

Three months passed like this. I lost thirty pounds. I lay on top of my bed for days at a time. My doctor gently broached the idea of institutionalizing me. I told him, honestly, that I did not care one way or the other.

And then one afternoon, as I lay on top of my bed, I fell into a deep sleep, deeper than I can ever remember experiencing. When I awoke, almost twenty hours later, I knew that I had turned the corner. Less than two weeks after that I was feeling like my old self again—perhaps, it seemed, even better. Somehow clearer, purer.

Leaving Sarasota, I traveled north on Interstate 75 until it met Interstate 10, and then I headed west for Albuquerque, home of my former patient Seth Waterson. This is a part of the country I had never seen before—Alabama, Mississippi, Louisiana, Texas, New Mexico. I drove at a leisurely pace, occasionally switching to secondary roads and passing through dusty towns that looked like Walker Evans photographs from the depression.

Since that awful episode three years ago I have tried to understand what happened to me then and why. There is part of me that, justifiably or not, remains deeply ashamed of myself about it. Not of the depression itself but of its apparent cause. Is my attachment to the material world so consuming that all it takes to push me over the edge is a major financial setback? Is my ego that flimsy, that petty?

As a psychoanalyst I have always believed that people who jump out of windows when they lose their fortunes are people who have failed to find transcendent meaning in their lives. And *that* is their real failure. If they had fully developed eros— a mature capacity to love their families and friends, the earth, life itself—they would not have attached their total self-worth to money. Could an underdeveloped capacity to love have been the nature of my own failure?

And of course, there was a deeper question that had surfaced to confound and disturb me: For all the years of my own analysis, did it turn out at the age of sixty-five that I had missed something crucial about myself? Could it be that *the Analyst* didn't really know who he was himself?

As I drove through this sultry southern landscape, I realized that that question, too, was a fundamental reason for this journey I had embarked upon, this pilgrimage in search of story endings. My training supervisor, Erich Fromm, wrote this in *Zen Buddhism and Psychoanalysis:* "The analyst analyzes the patient, but the patient also analyzes the analyst, because the analyst, by sharing the unconscious of his patient, cannot help clarifying his own unconscious. Hence, the analyst not only cures the patient, but is also cured by him."

I journeyed on to Albuquerque.

SETH WATERSON was in the midst of a crisis when he first came to see me in the fall of 1963. Married only three months, he had abruptly become impotent, and his wife was now threatening to leave him if he did not start "functioning properly."

A tall, soft-spoken man of twenty-five, Seth had the haunted look of a Goya figure. The cast of his hooded eyes, the hunch of his shoulders, the heaviness of his movements all suggested a deeply depressed young man. To my surprise, he had been a well-established young filmmaker, a line of work that I reflexively associated with brashly confident men.

"It's not just this thing with Edith [Seth's wife] that's killing me," he told me in the first few minutes. "It's the fantasies, those awful fantasies. They've come back to haunt me again."

"Tell me about them," I said.

"You don't want to hear them," he replied. "They're too ugly."

"Let me decide that, okay?" I said—mildly, I thought.

Seth winced, as if I had challenged his basic judgment. Clearly the duress of his impotence had made him acutely sensitive to anything resembling criticism. Or was it the other way around?

"You'd be surprised what I hear in here," I said gently. "Nothing human shocks me."

Seth took a deep breath and let it out slowly.

"All right, you asked for it. There are two kinds of fantasies, and they both turn me on." He began matter-of-factly. "The most exciting of them is the Bleeding Woman fantasy."

The image Seth proceeded to describe to me in grisly detail was indeed ugly, a classic male sadistic fantasy. In it he binds a naked woman in a harness, then inserts a glass tube into her jugular vein. Next, he slips a metal pole inside her vagina, which arouses her, but as soon as she becomes aroused, she starts to squirt blood out through the neck tube. The more aroused she becomes, the faster her heart beats, the more blood spurts out of her. She is in utter terror, caught between sexual ecstasy and her imminent death.

"When I imagine the blood streaming down her breasts, I get really excited," Seth said. "I start masturbating, and finally I come with the sound of her screams ringing in my ears."

Seth had become significantly more animated as he described this fantasy, and I found myself carefully hiding the anxiety which this aroused in me. It was not the fantasy itself that alarmed me; God knows, I had heard other odious fantasies within these four walls. No, what worried me was the fact that Seth had emerged so completely from his depression while he relived the fantasy; he seemed to come back to life.

Many people think of the opposite of depression as elation or a sense of well-being. Not me. I see depression as a form of psychic and emotional death and its opposite as vitality. Sadism, grotesque as it is, can be a way for a person to feel alive when other ways of feeling alive are not available to him or her. It is literally a perverted route to vitality. In this way it is similar to some drug addictions: For the addict, being "high" is often the only way he can contact the élan vital—the life-force. But also like a drug addict, the sadist has to keep upping his "dosage" for it to keep working. I could already imagine a time when fantasies alone would not be enough to pull Seth Waterson out of the depths of his deadly depression. He would then have to up the "dosage," and that could be extremely dangerous for him and for the people around him.

I asked Seth about his other recurrent fantasy, and he proceeded to describe the flip side of the first, a classic masochistic fantasy: "I am tied by the ankles, blindfolded, with a pear in my mouth. I'm attached to a giant succoring machine that is capable of satisfying every conceivable desire. This machine is linked to all my orifices, cares for all my needs. The machine says, 'Come, little boy. Come.' I'm supposed to have an orgasm, but I realize that I'll be killed by the machine if I do. I'll be killed right at the point of orgasm. This machine has total control over me."

Little wonder that this was a man with an impotence problem; an erection could kill him.

"I've had these fantasies since I was fourteen," Seth blurted to me. "It's who I really am, you know—the person in those fantasies."

"How do you mean?"

"Ugly. Cruel. Unlovable."

There was something so terribly pained in the way Seth uttered these words that I instinctively felt just the opposite must be true of him, that buried inside his sadomasochistic personality was a true lover of beauty and kindness—an eminently lovable human being. For better or for worse, I am apt to feel that about most of my patients.

"You must have quite a mother," I said.

For the first time since he had entered the office, Seth raised his eyes to mine.

"What makes you say that?" he responded, looking surprised.

I let my smile show as I thought of his lethal "succor machine" and its command to "Come, little boy. Come."

"Just a wild guess," I replied with just a suspicion of a wink.

For a split second Seth smiled, too, as if we were sharing a private joke. And then he sank directly back into his lifeless depression.

"Tell me about her," I said softly.

It took a great deal of coaxing, but when Seth finally did begin to tell me about his mother, the story flowed out of him virtually nonstop for the next several sessions. Seth's mother was one of the most monstrous parents I had ever heard described to me.

Amelia Anderegg Waterson McGruder Bailey was a dedicated narcissist as well as, apparently, a gifted intellectual; she was well read in philosophy, psychology, mythology, and the major literatures of four languages. Although not particularly physically attractive, she almost always had a man living with her—a man whom she would criticize and revile until he finally found the strength to leave her. Seth's own father, the first of her three husbands, left when Seth was not quite two years old.

"In my teens, when I finally got a chance to talk to my father, he told me that he remembered coming home night after night and finding me hungry, strapped to the sink or a chair in filthy diapers. He said there were feces smeared all over me."

Seth vividly remembered the clips and straps with which his mother tethered him.

"There was this harness that went around my chest and over my shoulders—like the kind you put on a bulldog. And then there was a leash clipped to the back so I couldn't reach around and free myself. Mother tied the other end to whatever was handy—the sink, the crib, the clothesline, the bicycle rack outside the library while she was inside studying."

I made no effort to conceal my expression of utter disgust as Seth related this to me, and he immediately reacted with "Listen, lots of mothers did that in those days. You bought those harnesses in baby stores, not in pet shops, you know. She did it for my own safety."

Heaven help him, he was defending her! I was getting my first inkling of what I was up against here.

"Did you ever manage to get free?" I asked in as neutral a voice as possible.

Seth eyed me suspiciously a moment, then brightened.

"Yes, once," he replied. "I chewed through the rope with my teeth and then took off down the street."

"Did you get far?"

"No. It was like that old joke: I couldn't run away because I wasn't allowed to cross the street."

That old joke struck me as emblematic of what I sensed already was Seth's basic problem: He could not escape from his controlling mother because he still felt he needed her permission to leave.

Amelia's husbands and lovers came and went throughout Seth's childhood.

"It always started out like this was the love of Mother's life, but within weeks Lila [his half sister] and I would start hearing them scream at each other in the bedroom. Lila would get terribly frightened, and I'd have to comfort her."

"How would you do that?" I asked.

Seth shrugged. "I'd just tell her that Mother didn't really mean it."

"Didn't mean what?"

"You know, like she didn't really mean it when she yelled, 'I'm going to kill you!' "

"Did she often yell that at her lovers?"

"Yes. I remember hearing that a lot."

"Didn't that scare you, too?" I asked.

Seth hesitated.

"A little, I guess," he whispered.

I asked Seth about his relationships with the succession of men who shared a bed with his mother.

"Frank was my favorite, I guess. He was Lila's father, and he occasionally made an effort to do father-type things with me. Took me fishing, took me to a couple ball games. None of it was exactly my thing, and I think he was kind of disappointed with me. Anyway, he was gone in a couple of years."

"Who was your unfavorite stepfather?" I asked.

Seth looked down at the floor.

"I don't know. It's like anything else: You click with some people and not with others."

I wasn't buying that. I was sure more was going on here than just the vagaries of personal taste.

"Okay, who didn't you click with, then, Seth?" I asked pointedly.

Seth suddenly raised his head and glared at me with venomous eyes. "Get off my back, will you, Doctor? Stop trying to push me!"

I gazed steadily at Seth. Should I back off? From the start I had been more directive and reactive with him than I usually was with patients. I had chosen this route not simply because Seth was in the middle of a crisis but because his depression had made him so inert that I felt he needed a "push" to start moving in any direction. But there was a clear risk involved in being too aggressive with him: He could completely withdraw from me in anger and distrust, and then my role as therapist would be seriously compromised. I was obviously getting perilously close to that point. Still, I had a hunch, and I didn't want to let go of it.

"What did he do to you, Seth?" I asked softly.

Seth's eyes immediately filled with tears, and his thin torso started to tremble. As I so often had to do over the years, I strenuously resisted my instinct to rise from my chair and embrace the suffering human being across from me. Seth whimpered quietly for several minutes.

"You bastard!" he hissed when he was finished crying.

I waited.

"His name was Bill," he said finally. "He was husband number three. I was twelve. He only tried it twice. The first time Mother was away and he just climbed into my bed and pressed his penis against my belly. But he was so drunk that he fell asleep before he could do anything. The next time Mother was home, and he came into my room and said, 'Your mother wants me to teach you about sex. Show me how you masturbate and I'll tell you if you're doing it right.' I ran into the closet and kept the door closed tight until he left."

I shuddered inwardly. This was 1963, before child sexual abuse stories were regularly recalled and related in therapy, let alone routinely recounted on television talk shows.

"Do you think your mother really sent him in to instruct you about masturbation?"

"Probably, yes," Seth replied. "I know she wasn't happy about my masturbation."

"How did she even know about it?"

"From the sheets of my bed. The stains."

"And she told you not to do it?"

"Oh, no. That's not how Mother does things. No, one night at dinner she stood up and announced that she was sick and tired of scrubbing my sheets. She said if I was going to masturbate, I should at least do it right and not mess up the sheets. She said I should do it with a Kleenex."

Incredible! In one masterstroke Seth's mother had managed to invade his privacy, humiliate him in front of his half sister and current stepfather, and make his emerging sexuality *a burden to her!* And all of this without even giving Seth a moral pronouncement to rebel against. No, Mother wasn't saying that masturbation was bad, just that he was *doing it wrong!*

Seth's mother's egocentrism was so complete that she responded to virtually everything her son did as if it were deliberately directed at her. If Seth failed to put his plate in the sink, she would say, "You leave a mess around here just to spite me." If he brought home a bad mark from school, she would say, "You are purposely trying to humiliate me, aren't you?" Once, when he came down with the flu during Christmas vacation, she accused him of deliberately sabotaging her favorite holiday.

But like any talented manipulator, she was adept at lavishing extravagant praise on her subject just when he had given up all hope of pleasing her.

"I remember one time when everything was falling apart for me," Seth told me. "It was the end of the year—sixth grade—and I'd been left back. There was this gang of kids who were tormenting me every day on the playground—beating on me and forcing me to eat stuff like ants and moths. This was around the same time that Bill was trying to . . . you know. I remember at the time the only way I could put myself to sleep was by imagining I was standing in front of a firing squad.

"Anyhow, I remember this one night I was sitting on the floor of my bedroom with a black crayon in my hand, just absently tracing squiggles on a piece of paper, when Mother came in. My heart was pounding. My God, what had I done now? She looked down at the piece of paper. Had I gotten some crayon marks on the floor? Was I wasting paper? Mother suddenly smiled and said, 'You're a genius! No, truly, it's an ocean. I can actually feel it—feel the movement of the waves. What feeling! This is exactly the way Picasso started, darling!' "

It was Amelia who was the genius—a genius at solidifying her power over her helpless little boy.

"You are one in a million," she would tell him repeatedly. "But you are nothing without me."

No wonder the idea of separation from Mother would panic him.

I did not learn until our fifth session that Seth had remained living with his mother right up until he married Edith, now five months ago. In fact, his courtship of Edith had been carried out clandestinely, and his mother heard about Edith only after Seth was married to her.

During this initial four months of therapy I had deliberately tried to limit our discussions of Seth's current crisis: his impotence and his wife's threats to leave him. Whenever he did mention his problem, he immediately sank back into a mute depression, and the silence could last the rest of the hour. I knew there could be no quick fix for him. Neither his unresponsive penis nor his relationship with Edith was his fundamental problem; they were just the symptoms that had brought him into my office. Seth told me that his sadistic and masochistic fantasies had not abated in the least since we'd started working together. In fact, he said that he had recently taken to buying pornographic magazines and drawing pictures of bloody mutilations over the photographs of naked women. In short, Seth had started to up his dosage.

THREE YEARS before Seth became my patient, I went back to school. Although I already had a doctorate in psychology, I had become gradually aware of the fact that if I wanted to do the kind of in-depth work with my patients that I felt they needed, I would have to train in psychoanalysis. My first and only choice for this training was the William Alanson White Institute, then as now in the vanguard of neo-Freudian therapy with an openness to unorthodox perspectives, including those of existentialism and Zen Buddhism. Above all, I was attracted to the White Institute because the two analysts whose writings spoke most powerfully to me were currently teaching there: Rollo May and Erich Fromm. I was four months into Seth's therapy when I received word that I was to begin one-on-one training with the supervisor I most desired, Dr. Fromm himself.

To say that I was nervous would be to understate the case seriously. Our first two-hour session was scheduled to begin at 10:00 A.M. on a Monday. That morning I was up at 5:00, had dressed and breakfasted by 6:00, and was out pacing Riverside Park and talking to myself by 7:00. The case I planned to present was Seth's, and to that end I had brought with me most of my records on him as well as tape recordings of two of our therapy sessions and a rather heavy reel-to-reel tape recorder-player. (This was before the days of cassettes and microelectronics.)

I arrived at Fromm's building on Riverside Drive a good fifteen minutes early, took the elevator up to his penthouse only to discover that there was no waiting room, just a hallway with no chairs and barely any light. I stood there, several feet in front of his door for the full fifteen minutes, never once setting the tape player down. When Dr. Fromm opened the door at ten on the button, sweat was dripping down my face onto my collar. Fromm smiled and ushered me inside.

Physically Fromm was hardly an imposing figure. Rather short and somewhat plump, he was modestly dressed in open shirt, tweed jacket, and dark trousers. His thick graying hair was combed straight back from his squarish face, and he wore rimless bifocals that seemed to emphasize the bushiness of his eyebrows. But the man's famed intensity—his highly focused energy—was instantly palpable. I felt it in the powerful intelligence that shone through his eyes, yet it also seemed to radiate from his entire face; for lack of a better term, I would say that Erich Fromm had a robust aura.

Once inside Fromm's small, book-strewn office, I remained standing, searching the walls for a socket in which to plug the recorder. Fromm watched me a moment, looking rather bemused, and then said, "Tell me, Dr. Akeret, what do you know of narcissism?"

I stared back at him, the recorder still in my hand. My God, it was a test! If I didn't pass, he would surely turn me right back out the door to make room for a better-prepared student.

"Yes, narcissism." I fumbled. "Self-absorption, a total immersion in one's own—"

"Let me tell you a little story." Fromm interrupted, his eyes twinkling. "When I was a young man studying in Frankfurt, I was constantly worried that I would make career choices that would set me on the wrong path and I'd never be able to get back on track again. I could be quite obsessive and obnoxious on this subject. Well, one day I said to my uncle, 'What will become of me?' and my uncle instantly replied, 'You, Erich? You will become an old Jew!' "

He burst into laughter, and in a moment I was laughing with him. Then he gestured to the chair beside his desk. I set down the tape player and sat, my head spinning. What had just happened here? In a single little anecdote Fromm had shown me the folly of trying to impress him with my preparation and earnestness. I was here to learn, not to be his star student. He had managed to tell me this in a self-effacing, humorous story without a hint of direct criticism. What's more, in laughing together, we had made immediate emotional contact. Thus began my training with Dr. Fromm.

I proceeded to tell him about Seth, his presenting problem, his background, and my work with him to date. Fromm listened enthusiastically, nodding his head, shaking his head, smiling, frowning, hitting the edge of his desk with his open hand. He reacted as if he had never heard such a bizarre and compelling story in his life, although I knew very well that he had literally heard thousands of similar stories in his professional career. But of course, that was the point: No two stories—no two *persons*—are the same. One must always focus on the patient's individuality, not see him as a "type" or as an example of a particular psychological syndrome. Again Fromm was not offering this to me as a lesson; he simply believed that this was so and was reacting accordingly.

When I finished my presentation, he said, "What a battle you have on your hands, Doctor. I wish you great strength."

He turned in his chair and gazed for a moment out the window onto the Hudson. It was early April. The sky was bright; the trees in the park were just budding. Then he turned back to me.

"Sadism is always so sad, don't you think? Such a sad attempt to compensate for powerlessness. A sad attempt to transmute impotence into omnipotence. Your patient must have lived a painfully curtailed life with this monstrous mother of his. I see it everywhere I look in the world—a will to destructiveness as the result of an unlived life."

I wanted to reach in my pocket for my pen and notebook so that I could jot down his words and study them later, but I knew that that was not the way Fromm wanted me to learn from him. The ideas were important, but the immediacy of our responses to each other was more so.

"What really strikes me about Seth's fantasies is how mechanistic they are," Fromm went on. "A bloodletting *machine*, an orgasm *machine*. In his fantasies he is an object, not a living human being. It is so thoroughly necrophilic; the man is trying to objectify himself out of existence."

A couple minutes later he asked me, "Do you think in his core he truly wants to escape from this mother fortress of his?"

"Yes, I really believe he does," I said, then added, "That's just my feeling, of course."

"*Only* your feeling, Dr. Akeret?" He laughed. "Tell me, what else do we have to go on in our work—signs from God?"

A moment later he said, "Your patient knows that it all begins and ends with this terrifying mother, doesn't he? He knows it, and yet he doesn't know it at all."

"Exactly," I said.

"It is not easy," Fromm said, shaking his head back and forth. "Sometimes telling a patient that he is angry with his mother is like telling Hamlet that he is not fond of his stepfather. The patient has to feel it in his blood to really know it."

Fromm asked me about Seth's dreams, and I automatically reached for my records. Seth was a prolific dreamer with great recall, and I had carefully recorded all the dreams he'd told me. Fromm made a dismissive gesture with his hand.

"Just one that you remember," he said.

I recounted the most recent dream Seth had told me. It was just a snippet, really. In the dream Seth strikes his mother with all his might, but she doesn't feel a thing. After a couple more of these hits, the mother turns to Seth and says, "That's wonderful, darling! Show your anger! Do it more!"

"Marvelous!" Fromm cheered. "What do you make of it, Dr. Akeret?"

The dream's meaning seemed eminently clear to me.

"It shows how powerless—how impotent—he feels in relation to his mother. Hard as he tries, he can't make a dent in her," I said.

"But what about *you?*" Fromm said. "How did you fare in this dream, Dr. Akeret?"

I gazed back at him perplexed. I didn't see myself in this dream anywhere.

"Oh, she's very clever this woman, even in his dreams," Fromm said. "This business of 'Show your anger! Do it more, darling!'—why, it's a devastating parody of psychotherapy itself. A parody of *you!* She's mocking you, Doctor. She still has all the power over him, and she knows it. And so, obviously, does Seth."

He leaned toward me in his chair.

"The battle lines are drawn very clearly, Dr. Akeret," he said. "It's like the wager God made with Satan for the possession of Job's soul. And the devil always starts with an advantage—the advantage of not being restricted by moral considerations."

A few minutes later I glanced at my watch for the first time since I'd entered Fromm's office. It was eleven forty-five. I only had fifteen minutes left, and there was a question I needed to ask.

"Do you think Seth could become really dangerous?" I asked. "Act out his fantasies and actually hurt someone—his wife perhaps?"

"Yes, that's a real possibility, I'm afraid," Fromm answered seriously.

"My God, what can I do?" I blurted.

"Help him choose life," Fromm replied quietly.

We both remained silent for a moment. It was time to leave. Fromm smiled warmly at me.

"So, Doctor," he said, "what have you learned about yourself from your patient?"

I thought I had misheard him.

"About him?" I fumbled.

"No, about *yourself*, Akeret. What you learn about him follows from what you learn about yourself."

For some reason unknown to me, my dream of a few nights earlier suddenly popped back into my consciousness. It was, I thought, the most transparent dream I'd had in years, and when I'd awoken, I was pretty sure that it had been stimulated by my recent sessions with Seth. In the dream I row a dinghy across a stormy channel to a little one-room weather-worn cottage on an island. Inside, in the middle of this room, is a large, soft bed, and lying in it is my mother in a nightgown. She motions for me to join her in the bed, and in great excitement I dive under the covers with her.

When I told the dream to Fromm, he clapped his hands together enthusiastically.

"Wonderful! I do believe you will be able to help this poor fellow," he said. "You are already swimming together in the same waters."

"The Oedipal waters," I said, smiling.

Fromm became intensely serious again. "There is a portion

in the Talmud that speaks of such dreams," he said. "It says that a man who dreams of watering an olive tree with olive oil has incestuous desires. But a man who dreams of sleeping with his mother is seeking after knowledge."

At noon I walked out into the sunshine feeling positively high. I was so bursting with energy that rather than head directly home, I walked over to the park and, tape player still in hand, bopped along the path, grinning like a schoolboy.

Seth had an appointment with me later that afternoon, and I found myself eagerly awaiting him. When he arrived, I sensed immediately that he was even more depressed than when I'd last seen him.

"So, how are things going at home?" I greeted him.

Seth shrugged, said nothing.

"How's your sex life going?" I asked. I certainly had not planned to say that. Yet it suddenly felt wrong to keep avoiding that topic, somehow unauthentic, disrespectful, as if by not mentioning Seth's impotence, I were ultimately engaging in a dishonest dialogue with him, and a patronizing one at that.

"What's wrong with you today, Akeret?" Seth shot back.

"Nothing at all. Why?"

"You don't seem yourself," Seth said petulantly.

"Oh, I am myself today," I answered. "Maybe even a bit more so."

I meant it. My session with Fromm had somehow empowered me, empowered my faith in my own intuitions.

"Well, there's still nothing doing, if that's what you want to know," Seth replied, spitting out the words contemptuously. "I'm still soft as a baby."

Interesting simile, I thought.

"So you've tried again to make love to Edith?"

"Of course. What do you think I'm talking about?"

"And that's really what you want to do with her: *make love?*

Even with all her threats of leaving you if you don't perform for her?"

"Jesus Christ, Akeret, you don't get it, do you? That's *why* I want to make love to her—so I won't lose her!"

I looked steadily into Seth's eyes. "I don't think you're impotent, Seth," I said. "I just think your penis has pride. It refuses to perform on demand. And to tell you the truth, I respect it for that."

Seth gazed back at me incredulously. I am sure that his first thought was that I'd gone completely around the bend. But I had just uttered what I truly believed—not a whim, not even a calculated therapeutic ploy. And this day I was more sure than ever that the greatest encouragement I could offer Seth—the best way I could help him "choose life"—was by speaking the absolute truth as I perceived it.

Neither of us spoke for several minutes. In that time I saw a succession of radically varied emotions swim across Seth's face: shock, sorrow, relief, and, lastly, a hint of strength. I had the distinct sensation that some of Fromm's empowerment had already been passed along.

"I've been having this new fantasy lately," Seth said at last, his voice low. "I take out this old straight-edge razor and I slice off my cock right at the base. I don't bleed or anything. It heals over instantly. And then I get this tremendous feeling of relief, like they can't get me anymore."

"Who can't get you anymore?"

"Edith. My mother. They can't criticize me anymore. Can't tell me how inadequate I am anymore. If I don't have a cock, how can they expect anything of me? I'm finally one of them! *I finally have the power!*"

What an amazing and devastating fantasy! In spite of myself, I instantly imagined recounting it to Fromm. Which is what I did within minutes of entering Fromm's office at our next session.

"Ha! You could start a revolution with that story!" Dr. Fromm exclaimed. "It turns classical theory upside down. What we have here is a man suffering from *no*-penis envy! *Castration* envy!"

A moment later he said, "Do you really think his penis has pride? Or do you think his penis is working—rather, *not* working—for his mother? It seems to me that Seth married Edith as an act of rebellion against his mother. But he didn't really have the power to go through with it. That woman still has him tethered in a harness, and he is terrified of escaping from her. Terrified that he cannot live without her. So he set his rebellion up for failure. Doomed his marriage from the start. First, I believe, with his choice. From what I am hearing, Edith is not a fitting partner for him. But to make absolutely sure his escape-marriage failed, he became impotent. Perfect sabotage. Mother wins hands down. Now he can go running back to her with his penis in his hand. To the winner go the spoils."

In less than two sessions Fromm had seen through to the basic dynamic that connected Seth's impotence with his marriage and his mother—a dynamic that I had not completely fathomed in a half year of working with Seth.

"Was it a mistake to say to him that I thought his penis had pride?" I asked.

"Not at all," Fromm replied. "You believed it, and he knew that. What's most important is that he felt your attention, your aliveness to his being. That's why you so thoroughly engaged him with that comment. I don't believe he would have told you his castration fantasy otherwise. But there is one thing you should be wary of, Dr. Akeret. There is a touch of the Swiss preacher about you. The evangelist. That's appealing, but it can also be very dangerous. Don't let Seth think you have your own ego invested in the outcome of his therapy. That's one pressure he doesn't need."

Near the end of the session Fromm and I discussed my future strategy with Seth.

"Try to work both sides of the street," Fromm said. "On the one side, Seth must truly feel how malignant his mother's hold on him is. And on the other, he has to begin to taste an alternative way of being. A way of being where he doesn't have to castrate himself in order to survive."

When I was at the door about to leave, Fromm grasped my arm. "Don't you wish we could tell Dr. Freud about the man with *no*-penis envy?" he said.

I smiled.

"Ah, well." Fromm sighed. "He would probably not find it amusing anyhow."

Despite my new grasp of Seth's situation and my clarified strategy for approaching it, Seth and I made no progress at all in the succeeding several months. Seth became increasingly petulant, listless, and generally uninterested in therapy. Several times he threatened to quit therapy altogether. I never argued against this with him; I would just say that I hoped he had some alternative plan for dealing with his problems.

Then, one day near the beginning of our second year of working together, Seth came home from a day of filming to discover that Edith had moved out. She had left a note saying that she had run off with someone named Caesar, a man "who knows how to make me feel like a real woman, not a failure, the way you've made me feel ever since I married you."

Seth was quivering as he related this to me.

"All I can think about is finding this guy—this *Caesar*—and slicing off his balls! Then I'll take a red-hot poker and ram it up Edith's cunt! I'll seal her up forever so nobody else can get in!"

As soon as Seth had said this, he burst into tears. I admit to feeling quite relieved when he broke down; sad as they were to behold, his tears showed me that he really did not want to be the avenging sadist of his fantasies. I took it as an indication that he would not act his fantasies out—at least not right away.

Near the end of this session Seth quoted a line from Edith's farewell note that he had not revealed to me before. Edith had written, "I should have listened to your mother a long time ago."

"But I thought Edith never met your mother," I said.

"She never did," Seth answered. He stood, walked over to where he'd deposited his briefcase when he came in, and withdrew a large manila envelope. He handed it to me. "A year ago Edith received this letter from Mother. I didn't know about it until Edith left it for me yesterday."

I took a quick glance inside. The letter was handwritten on typewriter paper. It was a hundred pages long.

"May I hold on to this a bit?" I asked.

"Keep it!" Seth replied disdainfully. "I don't need it."

That night after I'd seen my last patient for the day, I took out Amelia's letter to her erstwhile daughter-in-law and began to read:

*Dear Miss Mote (I don't spell it "moat" since I trust that you are not this. I spell it the kind that is biblically in the eye of "my neighbor" and since I have removed the mote from mine own eye, I am by definition ready to remove the motes from the eyes of others).*

*I hate this, yet it has to be. I wish you had come forward yourself. If you were smart, you would have studied me, what my life was and why, looking for clues as to what you could expect your life to be with my son since family patterns repeat in unbroken chains. For contrary to what your operations seem to indicate, you cannot take a human being and shape him to your own taste. . . .*

Spellbound, I read through to the last brilliant, insane, venomous, incredibly literate page.

Over the next two months Seth sank even more deeply into his depression, rendering him virtually speechless during most of our sessions. On the few occasions that he did come to life at all, it was to report his latest grotesque sadistic fantasy of cutting up Edith or some nameless, faceless woman. I know that Seth continued his film work during this period, but how he managed that was a mystery to me. Several times I tried to broach the subject of his mother's letter to Edith, but he was totally unresponsive. He was getting thinner by the week.

During this period Dr. Fromm had departed for eight months to his alternate teaching position at the Mexican Psychoanalytic Institute in Mexico City. Several times I was on the verge of phoning him there to seek advice on the impasse I had reached with Seth, but at the last moment I would always decide against intruding. When Fromm returned to New York the following spring, I requested his first available hour.

"There is such an inevitability to the way his story unfolds," Fromm said after I'd brought him up-to-date on Seth. "All the springs were wound tight. Now the principals are simply playing out their parts. Not only Seth, but Edith, his mother— even perhaps this interloper Caesar. The marriage has broken right on schedule. Seth's escape is foiled. Now comes the defining moment: Will he let the tragedy continue uninterrupted or will he finally take responsibility for his own life?"

I told Fromm about the letter from Amelia that Edith had left behind, and when he expressed interest, I took it out to show to him.

"No, no, read it to me yourself, please."

Fromm listened raptly as I began to read. He rocked back and forth in his chair, clapped his hands several times, and twice asked me to reread portions. After I'd read about ten pages, he signaled me to stop.

"What a document of malignancy!" he cried. "It's classic. There is something about the written word that the spoken word can never offer. You can go back to it again and again. Study it. Take your time peeling away the layers. Perhaps Edith left this letter for Seth as a parting gift, not just as a parting shot. How have you used it, Doctor?"

"I, uh, I've studied it, of course," I began nervously. "But Seth's total withdrawal has made it impossible for me to—"

"Seth is a film director, correct?" Fromm interrupted.

"Yes."

"Have him read it aloud. Beginning to end. A dramatic reading. You understand, Akeret?"

At the start of our next session I handed Seth the letter and asked him to read it out loud. Seth gave me a pathetic look and set the letter down on the floor next to his chair.

"Read it, Seth," I said, raising my voice. "You're just killing time in here anyhow."

"I've already read it, thank you," Seth mumbled back.

"So read it again."

"What kind of games are you playing now, Doctor?" Seth replied. "Why don't you just admit that you can't help me?"

"Oh, I definitely *can't* help you," I retorted. "I thought you understood that."

"Is that your new alibi, Akeret?"

"No, that's *your* alibi," I said, reaching out for the letter. "Let me have that, I'll read it myself!"

Seth started to hand the letter back to me, hesitated, put on his reading glasses, and then began to read in a lifeless monotone: "*Dear Miss Mote . . .*"

I sat perfectly still, listening intently, trying to hear Amelia's words as if for the first time, all the while studying Seth's face, watching his eyes.

*I hate this, yet it has to be. I wish you had come forward yourself. If you were smart, you would have studied me. . . .*

Seth read rapidly, fluently, yet totally without affect.

*Have you ever considered me, my dear? What I was and am to my son? I am the soil in which Seth has his roots. Do you really believe you can transplant him to your own meager silt?*

Seth paused to wet his lips. When he began again, I detected the hint of an edge in his voice.

*Right now your relationship with Seth is in a very delicate equilibrium. I have purposely left it that way, but moment by moment you are altering this equilibrium. If I say nothing, do nothing, you will cut your own throat from ear to ear.*

Here Seth stopped and looked over the tops of his glasses at me. This was only the first of Amelia's "surgical" images. Seth looked shaken.

"I'm, uh . . . I seem to be running out of steam," he said quietly.

"Want me to take over for a while?" I ventured.

"Yes, please," Seth said.

I took the letter and began reading where Seth had left off.

*There is a world of difference between my son and my father. Seth lacks the capacity for anger and resentment that turned that man to iron. Seth does not have the spine, the focus, the will to forge himself into a Colossus.*

Without planning to, I had adopted an imperious, hectoring tone. The letter jumped from thought to thought, though always circling Topic Number One: Amelia herself.

*My second husband's psychiatrist told me twenty years ago, "You are that white thing, Desdemona, which all men yearn for, yet do not believe in, so that if they do find it, they must try to destroy it. That is why your husband treats you as he does." Tell me, Edith, who can fill the spot—such a big spot—that I held for Seth? Where could he ever find another Desdemona?*

The letter suddenly turned raunchy, as Amelia described a near-sexual encounter with an unwelcome female suitor.

*Listen, my dear, if lapping your nether lips and having you lap mine will add anything to my life, I'll let you know. Frankly, the flavor of fish isn't something I'm keen for even on Fridays! Anyway, if I feel the need of some tongue treatment, I'll get a dog. Their tongues are bigger and softer, and they're really expert with them!*

I glanced quickly at Seth. His lips were tightly pursed. He looked revolted.

"Your turn again," I said casually, handing the letter back to him.

He took it without hesitation and continued from where I'd left off.

*The handwriting is on the wall, my dear, dear unlady. If you succeed in focusing his whole life on you so that you are the Sun around which his life revolves, can you always guarantee to be a good, great, and true goddess? Do you really think I will hand over a human sacrifice to your altar? I, who have seen all the wonderful men of my family wrecked on it! I, who have operated such a sacrificial altar myself!"*

Seth had now pitched his voice into a shrill register. His eyes popped like a hyperthyroid's. The venom, the hauteur, the grandiosity of Amelia were all seeping through. Suddenly Seth stopped and took a deep breath.

"Let me take that again," he said to me in his own voice.

When he started the passage a second time, there was an odd tremor in his voice; it was a tremor of madness.

*I have been everywhere and seen everything and learned, learned, learned from everything. I have all the answers in my hands—all the important ones. I have answers that no one has yet, though they tumble all around just waiting to be picked up, as did dinosaur bones for God knows how many thousands of years. In fact, I wouldn't be at all surprised to get a Nobel Prize for what I am working on, because I will be doing in this field what Niels Bohr did in the field of physics. What field? I am sorry, my dear, it is too difficult to explain in terms that you might understand.*

Seth read on without pause for the next half hour.

*Maybe you could play cleverly enough to put a halter on Seth and blinders, too, but is that enough to hold him? I am the door through which you must pass to be able to start a life with my son.*

I looked at my watch. It was already past the hour. I had another patient waiting.

"We'll have to stop for now," I interjected quietly.

Seth looked dazed. He handed the letter back to me. We were only up to page 38.

For the first time in a year and a half Seth arrived early for his next session. I handed him the letter as soon as he sat down. He paused a moment, closing his eyes, taking several deep breaths. He was getting into the part.

*I have taken Seth right along with me, turn by turn, along the road of my thought, until last year when the turnings began to get too steep and demanding for him.*

The mad tremor was in Seth's voice again, but something new had been added to his interpretation of Amelia, something comic. He was pushing it into parody.

*Where are we now, my tarty one? All this has a point, really. I am tilting at your unconscious, as well as your conscious. I am communicating subliminally as well as liminally. I am drawing an indelible picture of myself on your helpless soul.*

Several minutes later Seth switched into a new voice, oddly familiar, but for a moment I could not place it. Then it hit me: He was doing Amelia as the lunatic Olivia De Havilland in *The Snake Pit.*

*I don't seem to detect much in the way of family ties around you, little lady. Didja ditch 'em so you could be free to live your own life? "Sleep around," this means, my little wench.*

Seth continued nonstop until the end of the hour, not once asking me to take over in the marathon. He slipped artfully from one voice to another—mad, comic, frenetic, diabolic—as he went from a passage of incredible grandiosity to a passage of morbid bitterness to a passage of raunchy sexuality. There was no need for me to comment; none of it required interpretation.

*Anyway, my poor girl, everything that you find in this letter is now in Seth's mind. I put it there. You would do well to keep in mind that superior intelligence manifests itself in a superior ability to perceive relationships—which are invisible to the ordinary mind. Now you may have the pleasure of watching my awareness of you, know you are being measured and evaluated in every single thing you do or say. There isn't any direction you can move, a single thing you can say that won't pull the rope tighter around your throat.*

"I'm afraid that's it for today, Seth." I interrupted. We were up to page 86.

When Seth arrived for our next session, I sensed in the clarity of his eyes and in the decisiveness of his movements that some new vitality had begun to animate him. He read through to the end of the letter and then, with barely a pause, turned back to the first page and started all over again.

*Dear Miss Mote . . .*

The voices he used this time were even wilder: a singsong falsetto, a Zen-like chant, a spitting, didactic German accent.

*I am a psychiatrist without portfolio, my dear girl. I know what I am doing at all times, the effect I am having, the effect I wish to have. And I am going to change psychiatry into something useful or discredit it entirely. I have the material to kill it with already. . . .*

Listening to Seth, I felt as if I were being drawn into an altered state. I closed my eyes. Images of a protean, devouring monster undulated before my mind's eye. Exaggerated as Seth's voices were, they had caught something essential about his subject. It was a consummate performance.

*Let me tell you about my son, Edith. He is a prince among men. He will be a king—if you get your sweaty little fingers off him.*

Seth read through the letter a total of five times over the next two and half months. Each time he entered my office, it was if we were setting sail together on a secret, hallucinogenic ocean. We swam together in Amelia's madness. Her venom coursed in our veins. During this time I probably said no more than a dozen words, most of them simply to alert him that our time was up. The change in Seth was gradual but unmistakable. It was like watching a man slowly flush a poison from his system, slowly come back to life.

At the conclusion of his final reading of the letter Seth pulled another manila envelope from his briefcase and handed it to me. Inside was a sheaf of pornographic photographs of women overlaid with red-ink drawings of nail-lined halters, gaping wounds, and spurting blood.

"Destroy these for me, will you?" he said.

"I'd be happy to," I said.

A few weeks after that Seth announced that he had made love for "the entire weekend" with a woman he met at a party. Then he said that he had decided to take a leave from his job to travel in the West for an indefinite period. He asked if he could phone me if he ever felt the need, and I said of course.

"Have you told your mother about your plans?" I asked him.

"Yes," Seth said. "She said it was a desperation move. That you can never escape yourself."

"And what did you say to that?"

"I told her I was lucky to be escaping with life," Seth said, smiling.

My rotation with Dr. Fromm had been over for some time, but I would occasionally run into him at the institute. Next time I saw him, I approached and told him how well his strategy of having Seth read his mother's letter had worked out.

"So, he finally got to know in his blood who she really was," Fromm said.

I nodded and told my teacher how grateful I was for his help in curing Seth.

"We never cure anyone, Dr. Akeret," Fromm said severely. "We just stand by and cheer while they cure themselves."

ARRIVING IN ALBUQUERQUE had a time-warpy feel after cruising through the dusty red-neck towns of Louisiana and North

Texas. The city felt a bit like San Francisco in the sixties over-laid onto a sprawling cowtown. I was particularly struck by the men I saw in the streets, strapping men in cowboy boots and leather vests with ponytails bobbing out from under their cowboy hats. They were Hispanic, Anglo, Native American, black, Asian, and they exuded a certain manly gentleness. Many, if not most, were people who had come to Albuquerque to get away from the pressure and clutter and claustrophobia of life in cities in other parts of the country. Everyone I spoke to in my few days there mentioned the sky when I asked why he or she had chosen to live in Albuquerque.

I had talked to Seth on the phone just twice in preparation for my visit to him, first to ask if he was willing to see me, then to accept his invitation to stay in his house that he had Express Mailed to me right after the first call. He said that he was eager to see me, that it would be great to "talk shop" with me.

Seth's house looks as if it had a life of its own. Set on the edge of the massive Sandia Mountains, it juts and sprawls around a wild garden. Flowers grow on every side and in window boxes hanging under all the first-floor windows. No sooner had I driven up in my van than out the front door streamed this remarkably handsome and healthy-looking family: Seth, his second wife, Marianne, their fourteen-year-old daughter, Mica, and nine-year-old son, Adam.

Seth, still slim, but now wiry and rugged-looking, had close-cropped salt-and-pepper hair, a ruddy complexion, and a warm smile. He strode right up to me and threw his arms around my shoulders.

"Welcome, Bob," he said, hugging me.

A moment later he introduced me to his family. Marianne said that she had heard a lot about me and that it was a plea-sure finally to meet me. As they led me in the front door, I noticed a small hand-lettered shingle partially obscured by a trumpet vine just above the doorbell. It said: SETH WATERSON, COUNSELOR.

Dinner was served on a cedar deck that faced the primal-looking Sandia Crest. Before we dug into a gourmet vegetarian meal, hands were reached around the table and the Waterson family sang grace in a round: "For health and strength and daily bread, we praise thy name, O Lord."

After the meal Mica brought out chai in ceramic mugs. Everyone fell quiet as the sun slid toward the crest. It was spectacular.

"Best sunset I've ever seen." Seth cheered as the sun sank behind a granite ledge.

His family laughed.

"He says that every night," Adam said.

"I mean it every night," Seth said, ruffling the boy's hair.

Later Seth built a fire in the fireplace in his study. We were alone. We sat in twig chairs facing each other.

"I've been anticipating this moment for a long time."

"You always thought we'd meet again?"

"One way or another," he said.

Seth took a deep breath, then began to tell me the story of the thirty years of his life since we'd last seen one another.

"Going west felt like a pilgrimage from the start. A pilgrimage to my *real* home. I bought an ice-cream truck and fitted it out as a kind of early version of an RV. Part Kerouac, part Ken Kesey, maybe with a little 'Route 66' thrown in; after all, I was a TV man. About all I knew about where I was going was what I'd read in the *San Francisco Oracle*. You remember that one? One of the first psychedelic rags."

I sat back comfortably. It was clear that I was in the hands of a talented storyteller.

"I arrived in L.A. forty days later only to discover that my one friend there had recently taken off for points unknown, so some friends of his suggested that I journey on to Santa Cruz to a spot called Holiday. This was a group of cabins along a secluded bank of the Santa Cruz River deep within the shelter and magnificence of the redwoods. It had once been a vacation retreat, but now it was the home of an extended family of people who wanted a place of their own where they could practice the lifestyle they were in the process of discovering.

"I arrived there on the warm afternoon of November twentieth, 1966. I wandered down the dirt road to the bank of the stream, looking for someone to introduce myself to. There, sitting on the rocks in the sun, were two very friendly young women. They never asked what I was doing there, just my name and where I was from. I'm sure they sensed better than I did myself that I was carrying one hell of an emotional burden with me and had been carrying it a long time. They suggested that I bathe my head in the cool water flowing by. I did that—for much longer than I thought I would—and then we all just sat there together while I cried. Then, with their calm encouragement, I began to breathe again. And for the first time the whole world seemed to be breathing with me.

"Holiday turned out to be my home for the next three years, and those proved to be the most impressive, beautiful, and crucial years of my life up until that point. The magic of that time and place provided the ground from which the rest of my life has blossomed. It sounds a bit trite these days, but I was reborn there. If learning to breathe is crucial, then finding a place that breathes—nature's gift to those willing to listen carefully—can jump-start an organism in coma."

Seth paused and smiled at me.

"The sixties could not have come at a better time for me, Bob. Everybody had permission to rethink his whole life and start over again. To create our own extended families inspired by love instead of staying trapped in the cancerous families we came from."

I nodded. Fromm certainly would have appreciated the way Seth had put that, I thought. It occurred to me that all three former patients I had visited so far had pulled up roots and taken off for new parts of the world at the conclusion of their therapy. Was there something about my work with them that had created a craving for such a radical "fresh start"?

"In typical societal chauvinism, people called what we were doing dropping out, but to us it felt like dropping in," Seth continued. "In a *Wall Street Journal* article I was listed among two dozen or so people in the New York entertainment industry who had deserted the ranks for 'hippyism.' Around that same time I was interviewed by some eager young sensationalist from 'Huntley-Brinkley.' I had a few choice acerbic things to say, but I don't know if the interview was ever broadcast. Blessing of blessings, we had no TV at Holiday.

"Later on I hopped around from one commune to another, and in 1969, at the age thirty-one, I found myself living in the branches of an oak tree in the Santa Cruz Mountains! I slept with the birds! I wrote songs, meditated, read, and generally rediscovered the more inner aspects of life. Astronauts were landing on the moon then, and judging by their reports, we were all discovering about the same truths.

"This period was punctuated with visits back to New York fueled by the illusion that I could successfully go back to the kind of work and life I had known there. It never came off. I was offered work immediately each time, but after a week or two I would find myself down at the Lincoln Tunnel hitching west. The difference between life in New York and the free feeling of living in California filled my heart with an unbearable sense of loss.

"I was planning one more trip back East when Mother did me an unexpected and crucial favor. At the time I was living in Satchidananda's ashram, trying to get a little more yogic order in my life, and I initiated an exchange of letters between Mother and myself. It was our first contact in six, seven years. Resolution was on my mind. I wrote a couple of conciliatory letters, which elicited several unusually restrained one-hundred-dred-page replies."

Seth laughed softly before continuing. "We made plans for me to visit for an extended period, but then I suddenly got offered a fabulous job in San Francisco. I called Mother to tell her my visit had to be postponed, and she instantly became furious, wild, crazy, the whole achingly familiar monster thing again. She disowned me on the spot and hung up.

"It was perfect, actually. A cosmic wake-up call. 'Hey, Seth, she's not going to change, get it? *You* are changing, but she never will, so get on with your life, okay?' Of course, I was supposed to call Mother back and beg to be forgiven, but I didn't. Never have. That's twenty-five years ago. It's sad that I cannot have a sane relationship with my one and only natural mother, but so it goes. It's not a tragedy. It's not even a gaping hole in my life. All kinds of wonderful people have filled my days and nights since then. I could not be luckier."

Seth fell silent for a moment. So far everything he had said about himself rang true for me. I certainly did not sense any gaping holes in his life, but there was one question I had to ask: "Were you ever haunted again by your fantasies?"

"That awful S-M stuff, you mean?"

"Yes."

"Not once, Bob," Seth said earnestly. "Truth is, I can't even look at violent movies anymore. I lost more than my desire for that stuff; I lost my tolerance for it."

I smiled.

"By the way, that job in San Francisco turned out to be a real kick." Seth went on. "A producer I knew had created a challenging project for me. I spent five very exciting and productive years on it.

"During this time I lived in a cavelike apartment south of Market with a sandblasting establishment right across the street. Then, in '68, a friend turned me on to a physical-psychological technique similar to Rolfing called Heller work. It is incredible stuff where you reach deep inside to where the soma meets the psyche. It requires training in massage, acupuncture, and acupressure. I took to it like a duck to water, and fairly soon I was an instructor myself. My first client was Marianne. No laughter, please. We fell in love over an acupuncture table!

"Marianne and I kept wanting to dig further and further, finding out everything we could about what it was to be human. What our emotional potential was. And, ultimately, what our spiritual possibilities were, too. My approach to self and learning is like a spiritual kamikaze. I've got to fling myself headfirst into everything. We went into Gestalt and Reichian therapy, then into rebirthing. We took a course in Sufi dancing, one in akido and another in kendo. I went on a three-day guided LSD meditation. We both did some sessions in Feldenkrais and some in primal scream. Marianne studied a lot about herbal and flower healing. I studied shiatsu massage. There's hardly anything in the catalog of holistic health that we haven't at least had some contact with. I'm sure this all sounds like a hoot to you, Bob. But I don't regret any of it. The benefits in knowledge and personal development and especially in our ability to help others have been priceless."

Seth stood, threw another log on the fire, and sat down again. He grinned.

"I'm afraid I've omitted a couple of small miracles," he said. "You met them earlier—Mica and Adam. I can say without reservation that they've taught me more about living than all the therapies and courses put together. Still, maybe I am doing a better job of guiding them because I learned a thing or two from my own guides, starting with you, of course."

"Any lessons in particular come to mind?" I asked.

Seth shrugged. "It's never easy to put those kinds of things into a simple formulation," he said. "But at the point in my life that I was in therapy with you I had to make the most basic choice of all: whether or not to choose life."

I broke into a broad smile. "Did I ever actually use those words with you? *Choosing life?*"

Seth shrugged again. "I don't think so. Why?"

I told Seth about my training with Fromm and the advice he had given me about Seth's own treatment, how the notion of "choosing life" had been fundamental to it.

"Fabulous!" Seth cried, jumping up from his chair again. "Erich Fromm! Do you realize that *Escape from Freedom* is a seminal book in my life? I knew I had some kind of connection to that man the minute I started reading him. Now look at this! There is a straight line going from him to you to me. Talk about finding lost fathers!

"Let me bring you right up-to-date, Bob. For the last twelve years I have been a therapist myself. It's been an evolving thing, drawing on all that I have learned personally from life, piecing together themes and techniques from all the different disciplines I've studied. And I keep finding these commonalities that run through them all—from holistic healing to vision quests to chanting and whirling and fasting right back to psychoanalysis itself. They all begin and end with that same choice Fromm divined some fifty or sixty years ago. What's it going to be, folks? Necrophilia or biophilia? Do you choose life or do you choose death? Of course, it is never so clear and simple as that when you are deep in the abyss gasping for air. But that's where people like you and me come in. The psychic detectives. The spiritual kibitzers. The cheerleaders for life.

"God, I feel terrific!" He cheered. "I am really so glad you came out here, Bob. It feels so full circle, doesn't it?"

"Yes, it does."

"Hey! How about something to eat?"

I looked at my watch. It was a little after two in the morning. Incredible! We had been talking for five straight hours.

"I think I could eat," I said.

Seth whipped up a fabulous Mexican omelet filled with tomatoes, peppers, and a variety of cheeses. We put on jackets and took the food out to the deck, where we ate under the stars in silence. I felt at once wonderfully content and incredibly stimulated. Fromm was very much on my mind. For the first time since I set off from New York, I wondered what he would have thought of my pilgrimage. Not much, I decided. He would have seen too much narcissism in it. "What will become of me, Doctor?" "You, Akeret? You will become an old, itinerant Swiss preacher." Ha!

I wondered, too, what Fromm would make of all these New Age therapies and spiritual fixes that had mushroomed in the past thirty years. At the height of his own career he had sought out parallels between psychoanalysis and Zen Buddhism, much to the embarrassment of many of his more conventional peers. I could hardly believe that Fromm would fault someone like Seth for his ideological impurity, certainly not for his desire to experiment with new therapeutic techniques. But would he have suspected these postsixties therapists of a kind of spiritual faddism? Of encompassing such a great variety of cultural and conceptual modalities that a depth of personal experience was sacrificed?

There was another thought that had been dancing in and out of my mind as Seth spoke: It struck me that in several significant ways Seth was his mother's son. He spoke so fluently, with a flair for detail and arresting metaphors. That was a talent he'd obviously acquired from her. And then there was his gift for psychotherapy combined with his confidence that he could carry it off despite the fact that he did not have traditional training. I could not help thinking of Amelia's line "I am a psychiatrist without portfolio."

But if Amelia represented the ultimate in narcissism, manipulativeness, and destructiveness, Seth was very clearly the opposite—a lover, a giver, a healer, a builder. It seemed to me that Seth's accomplishment in transmuting his maternal inheritance into something so sublime represented a strong life-force.

I suddenly became aware that Seth was gazing seriously at me.

"I'm afraid my story's not over, not complete," he said softly.

I felt a little shiver pass along my spine. I said nothing.

"This is the story of the divine blight." He began with a painful smile. "In late 1983 I suddenly began to feel an appalling and deeply distressing torpor marked by a great loss of energy. I was horribly tired; my skin turned gray. I had this vagrant nausea, no appetite and started losing weight. Feelings of desperate hopelessness, a depressing sense of futility, and a crushing loneliness.

"For many days running, I just lay in the park on the grass thinking that I must surely be dying of some serious illness, probably cancer. That my life and the time with my family that I had worked so hard for were soon to be over. The desolation and sense of helplessness were overwhelming. Curiously, I wasn't frightened of the prospect of dying, just dreadfully sad. What was the importance of being in love with Marianne? What about seeing the kids grow into young adults? Where was the future of the work I had so looked forward to? Where was the fame I was supposed to achieve? My measure of immortality that would save me from the completely erased fate of some sixteenth-century tiller of the soil whose name and burial place are now totally lost to history?"

As Seth spoke, I barely moved. I had to make a conscious effort to keep steadily drawing in my breath. We were once again swimming together in the same waters.

"I saw a doctor, and he thought I might be mildly hypoglycemic, but that was all he could find. Life at home was very difficult. I could barely work. For a long time things only got worse. I began to have a heavy vibrating in my forehead and sinus area. I heard a strange singing-ringing sound almost constantly. I became hypersensitive to even mild temperature variation. And then this, in some ways the most awful reversal: I suddenly hated the sound of music! Music, the one constant in my life! I even found conversation maddeningly distracting and confusing. I was desperately tired all the time but could not sleep. I was paradoxically 'wasted' yet powerfully charged with some mysterious energy at the same time, although of course, I did not realize that yet. Not quite yet.

"My breath was bad; my teeth turned yellowish. I had dry heaves in the morning and was overtaken by this abysmal fear not that I *would* die but somehow that I was already dead. Some mornings I would just roll around on the floor, moaning and crying, before forcing myself to get ready for clients. Intestinal cramping and aching became a regular part of my life. I found it difficult to think, as if I inhabited a temporospatial warp which had me exiled one universe to the left of everybody else's. In fact, all I wanted to do—the only things I *could* do that brought me any sense of rightness—were meditate and work with clients. And my meditations began to be accompanied by incredible rushes of energy, some like clouds of champagne bubbles effervescing through the tissues. Energy seemed to be rising through my body and pouring with awful gravity down my face and the front of my body. I was in the care of both allopathic and naturopathic physicians, but nobody had any real answer to the puzzle of what was happening."

Seth abruptly sat forward in his chair, leaned toward me.

"I don't remember exactly when the answer came, Bob," he said in a half whisper. "But it was at once unexpected and appropriate, and it offered me a whole new realm of understanding. Because as it turned out, there was a strange kind of savage beauty to everything that was happening to me. It started with these weird vocalizations I would suddenly find myself doing: singsong warbles, wild cries and chants, long-held monotone bass notes like a Zen monk's trumpet. They resonated deep within me. And that was my first intimation of relief from my agony. I had this very profound sense of old burdens' being shed. It was as though I were experiencing a spontaneous and excruciating healing of ancient wounds. But it was obvious that somebody else was running the show with a single-minded ferocity, and I had virtually nothing to say about it. Sometimes I'd come out of these vocalizations feeling blissful, like I was totally stoned. I knew all I could do was hang on and wait for moments like that. I couldn't force anything. All I could do was wait and be ready to surrender to the next round of detoxification.

"Around this time I met up with an old friend from my commune days who is a serious student of Indian religions and who spends much of his time in India as a spiritual mendicant. He listened as I described what was going on with me, and then he said, simply 'It is the Shakti moving.'

"*The Shakti! The Serpent Power! The energy of enlightenment!* Everybody thinks that the process of 'clearing' is like walking down a garden path toward some effortless experience of bliss. And that the result of all this 'easy' work is simply a bubbly surge of soda water up the spine, culminating in a silly shower of sparks out the top of the head and a lot of psychedelia and smarts. Not so! The bliss is definitely there, but its attainment is a much tougher proposition.

"Of course, it became incredibly important for me to know more about all of this, since it was exerting an irresistibly powerful, even pivotal effect on my life. And since through some strange synchronicity my practice began to turn up people who were experiencing strikingly similar intense episodes and who were deeply worried because they could find no one who understood their situation. Some of them were seeing psychiatrists and were concerned that they were going mad."

"Didn't that thought ever worry you, too? That *you* were going mad?" I asked. It was my first question since Seth had begun the story of his "divine blight."

"Not once," Seth replied. "I let go of that particular concept—madness, psychosis—a long time ago, long before this episode hit me. I'm afraid your honorable profession has turned things upside down as far as the enlightened world is concerned. Psychiatrists can't get beyond the medical model that says if some part of the human being is not performing as usual, *as expected,* it must be sick! God forbid that they should think something wondrous is happening and that's why the person is behaving in this exotic way! Look, most doctors even think of childbirth as a pathological condition that results in a medical emergency!

"What I'm saying, Bob, is that what you call psychosis really means 'too many windows open.' Our fear of our own greater being is so overwhelming that we prefer 'lobotomy'— that includes Prozac and all the rest—to the risk of being all we could be. Stanislav Grof—you know, the last of the LSD researchers—says that the only real distinguishing feature between episodes of enlightenment and episodes of psychosis is that the psychotic places the power and the fault outside himself, while the former accepts ultimate responsibility for his condition and for the resolution of it. I'd go even further. I'd say that all the stuff we call nervous breakdowns, depressions, midlife crises, psychotic states, and probably most of what we think of as physical illness, all that stuff is what happens when the organism, in its struggle to block the Shakti, is either destroyed by itself or surrenders and is healed. The thing we've all got to remember is that in other societies when a person goes through one of these upheavals, he is considered to be in touch with extraordinary forces and realms of the mind. Not here, not now. Here, if you start shaking and quaking, they want to give you a pill to shut everything down, to *close* all the windows!"

Seth took a deep breath. Behind him the first refracted rays of the morning sun radiated over the mountaintop. We both were silent for several minutes.

"It happened to me, too," I said quietly.

Seth looked deeply into my eyes, waited. And then I told him about my own "blight" three years ago, my own battle with depression, despair, and sleeplessness. I told him how it had started and how ashamed I still felt when I thought that my attachment to money was its ultimate cause. When I had finished, we both fell silent again.

"Want to hear my guess, Bob?" Seth said finally.

"I do."

"I think you're an incurable gambler," Seth said with a sly grin. "In fact, I think you'd risk just about anything if you thought you could learn something from it."

I gazed back at him perplexed.

"I'd even wager that you rigged the whole deal." Seth went on. "Your whole cockamamy double-or-nothing investment scheme. You were hoping for a wipeout so you could get back to basics. So you could start doing a little digging of your own again. Start opening a few windows. You're not a hoarder, Bob, I know that much. I know how you live."

"But I had people to take care of," I protested. "Responsibilities—my children, my wife, my mother. And I let them all down."

Seth's face abruptly became serious again.

"That's what this is about, too, isn't it?" he said, gesturing to the space between us. "This ultimate follow-up study of yours. You want to know if you let us down, too, don't you? Your patients. You've just got to know, don't you, Bob? You just can't let go of it."

I felt strangely light-headed, dizzy. I suddenly recalled Fromm's warning me not to invest too much of my self in the outcome of my therapy, that it wasn't fair to either my patients or myself.

"Tell me." Seth went on. "How long was it after you healed from your blight that you thought of going on this trip?"

"Let me see—a couple months, I guess," I replied.

"Just coincidence, right, Doctor?" Seth laughed.

I gazed back at him, straining to get it.

"You're greedy, all right, Bob. But not for money. No, no, you're holding out for much bigger stakes than that. *You're greedy to find out if what you dedicated your whole life to has amounted to anything!"*

Seth was out of his seat, breathing deeply. He walked over and planted a hand on each of my shoulders.

*"Now who in his right mind would want to know a thing like that?"* he bellowed.

I stared up at Seth. Suddenly I was laughing, laughing hysterically, and so was he. I jumped up out of my chair. The sun had just hoisted itself over the mountain. Laughing like madmen, Seth and I started to dance together, a goofy hip-hopping around in a circle, our arms waving in the air like Icarus's wings as the sun flared at us in fiery streaks of red and gold. We started spinning, whirling, faster and faster. Oh, who was mentor? Who was student? Who was the guide and who was the guided? For one ecstatic, hallucinatory moment, I could swear that Dr. Fromm joined us on that deck in the Sandia Mountains, spinning, laughing, dancing, cheering. *Exalting!*

I SPENT TWO MORE DAYS with Seth and his family, but we did not "talk shop" again. I cannot say that I fully believed or even completely understood Seth's various theories of Shakti and "open windows." But I can say this with absolute certainty: I felt positively blissful for those two days in Albuquerque. And when I said good-bye to the Watersons early on a misty Tuesday morning, I was filled with life.

# F O U R

# Mary: Beware What You Desire

You have heard the commandment imposed on your
forefathers, "You shall not commit murder." . . . What
I say to you is this: everyone who grows angry with his
brother shall be liable to judgment.

Jesus, Matthew 5:21–26

Beware what you desire, for you will surely get it.

Bedouin proverb

WESTWARD TO CALIFORNIA, Bob Dylan's nasal tones
straining through the speakers of my van:

How does it feel to be on your own,
A complete unknown,
With no direction home,
Like a rolling stone?

I stayed high on my visit to Albuquerque all the way
through Arizona. Seth's joy in living was infectious. He had
managed to hang on to the best of the sixties and seventies—
the openness, the tenderness, the sense of life as an ongoing
improvisation. The magic, too. I envied him that.

Not that I had been immune to the power of those decades
myself. Although I hadn't taken off for points unknown in a
refitted ice-cream truck, the mythos of that period had crept

ineluctably through the door of my penthouse office on West End Avenue.

But for me, not all of it was magic.

A MONDAY MORNING in April 1974. I had eaten breakfast with my family, then sent the girls down the elevator and off to school. With a steaming mug of coffee in my hands, I set out on my morning stroll from home to work—twenty-five paces down the corridor from penthouse A to penthouse B. It was eight-fifteen; my first patient was due at nine. That gave me plenty of time to review the morning's patient records, sip coffee, maybe listen to some music on WQXR.

I knew there was something wrong the moment I fitted my key into the door. It was unlocked. I pushed; the door swung open. My office was in a total shambles. All the file drawers were open, files strewn on the floor from one end of the room to the other. The paintings were off the walls, one of the canvases ripped. The top of my desk had been swept clear—pens, blotter, phone, schedule book, all on the floor.

Right away I noticed two peculiarities of the break-in. First, my tape recorder, radio, and new typewriter were still there, albeit capsized on the floor. If this had been a burglary, the intruders certainly would have taken these items. Even if they had mistakenly thought I was an M.D. and were disappointed not to find a cabinet full of opiates, they would have at least taken the typewriter as a consolation prize; they could have easily fenced it for a couple days' worth of heroin.

Then there were the cigarette butts ground out in an open drawer of my desk, a good dozen of them. Someone (or two or three) had spent a fair amount of time in here. Smoking and probably reading. And the only reading matter here was my case records.

So it seemed a pretty good bet that my intruder was somehow connected to my practice—a patient, a relative or lover of a patient, or an enemy of a patient. And whichever of these he was, this person certainly had no affection for me. The ripped painting, the strewn paper, the toppled chairs were not simply the result of careless housekeeping while searching through my records. This was, to use the tepid psychological jargon that was then slipping into popular usage, an "act of hostility," and it was directed at me. Which is not to say that whoever broke in here wasn't looking for something specific in my case records.

Two patients sprang to mind immediately: Jack Noto and Beverly Griswold. Noto was a cocaine dealer with marital problems; Griswold was a young wife and mother who was in the process of divorcing her physically abusive husband. Noto had a rich variety of enemies, ranging from rival drug dealers to "narcs." All of these had much to gain from access to my files on him: names of Jack's customers, associates, sources—that is, if I actually possessed such files. But unknown to them, a condition of my work with Jack was that I would not keep any written records of our sessions; we had both assumed that that would make our work safer. As to Beverly Griswold, she had one specific enemy, and he had become mine, too: her husband, Rolf. Beverly was in the midst of a battle for full custody of their twin seven-year-old boys. Just three weeks prior to the break-in I had received a call from Rolf on my home phone at eleven at night. He was drunk. He blamed me for the breakup of his marriage and now for "stealing" his sons from him. Just before I hung up on him, Rolf threatened to kidnap my own children if he lost his.

There had been other phone calls, too, some as early as five in the morning, some as late as midnight. But in these my caller had not spoken a word. I could hear breathing on the other end; once I heard some music in the background, from a radio, I assumed. I had no idea who had made these calls. Rolf had been my prime suspect until he called that night and threatened me outright. After that call I doubted that he would suddenly revert to being coy. But it did seem more than likely that whoever had made the silent phone calls was the same person who had broken into my office last night.

Standing in the middle of my ransacked office, I felt the fury of being personally violated, yet at the same time I felt the rather mundane urgency to clean up quickly before my first patient arrived. There was no question of "preserving evidence"; I had no intention of calling the police. To begin with, my relationship with Jack Noto made that impossible. Maybe Jack's criminality made patient confidentiality a moot question legally, but it wasn't moot personally, I had made Jack a promise of confidentiality when I took him on, and I had no intention of breaking that promise. The same was true for my relationship with all my patients, including Beverly Griswold. I could not be helpful as a therapist to any of them if they did not trust me completely, and that meant that I could not do anything behind their backs, could not directly engage any third parties without their permission, and that included the police. There was one exception to this rule, and that was if I thought any of my patients was at immediate risk of physical harm. Then I could call the cops. But I had not reached that point yet. As to what to tell or not tell my patients about the break-in, I would deal with that later. Right now I had twenty-five minutes before my first patient, Mary McGinely, was to arrive for her nine o'clock appointment.

My wife, Ann, helped me put the room more or less back together. We simply stuffed the records back into the file cabinets; I would have to arrange them in order later, also check for what, if anything, was missing. The paintings that had not been damaged we rehung. Chairs were righted, desktop reset. Ann and I were still working when Mary showed up for her session five minutes early. She was standing in the waiting room, one hand on her hip, gazing through the open door of my office with a contemptuous expression on her face when I first noticed that she was there. I introduced her to Ann, but when Ann extended her hand, Mary did not take it. When we were finally alone, Mary said, "Funny time to be cleaning house."

As in most of our recent sessions, that was virtually all Mary said that day.

Mary McGinely was a nurse and midwife in her late twenties with a broad Irish face, clear blue eyes, long silky hair, and a plump body. When she had first come to see me some eight months earlier, she presented a timid and unassuming young woman, frightened of her own confused feelings and obviously suffering from extreme low self-esteem.

She sought my help after a series of inexplicable outbursts directed at her husband that had culminated in her smashing her husband's cherished guitar when he came home late one evening. She claimed that this burst of fury and destructive behavior were totally unlike her. She said, "I don't know what got into me. I'm losing control of myself."

During the first five months of therapy she was able to talk about herself, her background and her feelings, rather easily. She was the middle child of five in an Irish Catholic family that had lived in a working-class neighborhood of Hartford, Connecticut. She had been considered by one and all in her extended family to be the "plainest of the lot" and also the best behaved. From the start Mary lived the typically isolated, lonely life of a middle child in a large poor family. She had nothing special to call attention to herself—not the looks, talent, personality, or even a handicap or infirmity that would garner her parents' notice.

She remembered growing up in a series of hand-me-down dresses, shoes, and coats.

"Underwear, too," she told me. "That was the worst, I hated wearing my sister's hand-me-down panties. It seemed so—I don't know—not just unsanitary but too intimate. I'd line the insides of the panties with toilet paper so I wouldn't have to have contact with the cloth. Of course, that had its drawbacks, too; it irritated my skin terribly."

An added humiliation of wearing hand-me-downs was her older brother Jimmy's relentless comparisons of the way Mary looked in a particular article of clothing with the way her older sister, Connie, had looked in it.

"When I was a teenager, he'd always say things like 'Aren't you wearing that dress backwards? When Connie wore it, she filled out the front.' "

As was frequently the case in families like Mary's, the boys were valued more than the girls, especially if the girl had nothing more to recommend her than good behavior. No one cared about Mary's schoolwork, which was exceptionally good, because no one expected her to go to college or to have a career.

Mary told me that only now as an adult was she beginning to realize the full extent of the boy-girl discrimination in her family. Her mother had recently told her a story about how overtired she had been when Mary was an infant. Her pregnancy with Mary had been particularly difficult; she had vomited every day for eight months. There were many times, she told her daughter, when she thought the pregnancy would kill her. But the main problem, it seems, was that Mary's brother Jimmy, then four, still woke up crying every night and needed his mother to lift him out of bed and rock him back to sleep.

"[Mother] said that by the time I came around, she was totally exhausted. So after a couple of weeks she stopped breast-feeding me and just let me cry myself to sleep. I guess it worked; I must have stopped crying. But I don't know, Jimmy got four years, and I only got two weeks."

"Was your mother apologetic when she told you this story?" I asked.

Mary laughed bitterly. "Of course not," she said. "The whole point of the story was that I was supposed to feel sorry for *her*."

I was very quickly getting the picture of an emotionally deprived and, hence, extremely needy young woman. This raised the always perplexing question of how much to gratify her neediness with the approbation, praise, comfort, and love that a well-nurtured child would have received from her parents. The prevailing theory was to be extremely wary of feeding a needy patient's "emptiness"; the patient could never be satisfied, the theory went, and feeding her was only apt to cause her to grow hungrier and more dependent on the therapist. Furthermore, satisfying a patient's long-standing need for love and support hastens transference, the phenomenon wherein a patient displaces strong feelings toward someone in her past (usually a parent) onto the therapist. As one of my colleagues once wrote, transference "gives rise to some of the most intense, colorful, complex, perplexing, potentially destructive, and eventually most therapeutically useful aspects of the entire therapist-patient relationship."

I have always leaned toward the notion that well-placed and well-timed emotional "nourishment" has the potential to be wonderfully therapeutic, that it can fill the "holes" left by a deprived childhood—at least fill them enough so that one's choices in life are no longer seriously restricted by feelings of emptiness and unworthiness. The trick, of course, is to deliver this nourishment with clear limits, never to promise the patient more than one can deliver. This constitutes one of the most perilous balancing acts in all of therapy.

Like many families of that era, the McGinelys engaged in very little physical contact with one another.

"I don't even remember seeing my parents hold hands," Mary told me. "I sometimes thought all five of us were the product of immaculate conception."

Catholicism pervaded the life of the McGinely family, particularly affecting Mary.

"It was the only thing in the world that made me feel special," she said. "It was literally my salvation. God was on my side."

Mary adored the ritual and pageantry of her religion. She

also loved the orderliness of it, the pure distinctions between good and evil, the purpose in everything.

"I could feel God's power moving in me," Mary said. "I knew in my heart that faith could move mountains and that that, finally, was where my power lay. My only power."

There were many times when she believed that God had given her the gift of influencing events just by wishing them so. She recalled one time when she was late with a book report and she prayed for divine intervention. The very next day the sister who taught English fell ill with appendicitis, so Mary got the week's reprieve that she prayed for.

The price Mary had to pay for this power became abundantly clear to her: She had to be good. Very, very good.

"I was always such a good little girl—helpful, kind, never made any noise, never asked for seconds, never got angry. But I knew—and my priest knew—that that was just a cover for the bad girl hiding inside my skin. I was always having evil thoughts, and those, of course, are just as bad as evil actions. Worse, actually. So every week I'd trundle off to confession to expose all these black marks on my soul. And every time Father Bonnard would give me the same lecture about how all it takes is one evil thought to spread evil throughout the world. He'd say that the devil ate little girls' evil thoughts for breakfast and that's what made him so strong."

I asked Mary what kinds of evil thoughts she'd had.

"You know, just wishing bad things would happen to people," she said. "Like that Connie would lose her boyfriend. Or that the smartest kid in my class would get a sudden case of amnesia just before an exam. That sort of thing."

Mary's father had died of an aneurysm when she was ten years old. She did not tell me this until our third month of working together, a likely sign of denial. Yet she insisted that life had barely changed at all after her father died because he had never been home much anyhow; he had been a traveling salesman who was usually on the road.

"It was like he simply stopped visiting us on weekends," she told me. "We weren't used to setting a place for him at the table anyhow."

"Do you remember the funeral?" I asked.

"Yes." Mary sighed. "There was a lot of crying and everything."

"But not you."

"No," she replied matter-of-factly. "I've never been much of a crier."

Good girls probably didn't cry either. Too noisy. Too demanding.

"Did you miss having a father at home *before* he died?" I asked.

"A little, I suppose," Mary said.

I was not buying any of it but decided to leave the subject alone for the time being.

During those first five months of therapy Mary grew noticeably more content and less agitated. She reported that she had not had any more flare-ups at home, that, in fact, she and her husband felt closer than ever. They had decided to try to have a child and were making love happily and often.

I believed that much of Mary's new sense of security and well-being could be attributed to my "nourishment" of her, of providing a nonjudgmental ear to listen to her story. She came from a background that was fraught with judgments, and I was an all-accepting opposite of that. Clearly this had accelerated transference, a process she was probably familiar with, albeit unconsciously, from her early devotion to her priests; those fathers had been substitute fathers for her, too. The dreams she told me were fairly transparent on this score; I frequently turned up in them in a fatherly role, although often as an inept and distracted father.

But the combination of Mary's fast improvement and her obvious transference were cause for caution. There is a phenomenon known as the transference cure in which the patient is so eager to please her "newfound" parent that she willfully drops her neurotic symptoms. The only problem with this cure is that it is superficial and short-lived; when the symptoms inevitably return, they are as entrenched as ever.

Sometime in our fifth month of working together, Mary reported the following dream: She was back living in Hartford, and my office was next door to her house. I was very old, and she was in her early teens. When she came in for her regular session, I informed her that because of my advanced age, I was cutting back on my work load. I was keeping only special patients so I could devote more time to my family. And so I was dropping her. In the dream she was devastated. She was not "special" enough to keep my interest. Even when she recounted the dream to me in my office, she was obviously very upset, fighting back tears.

Around this same time Mary confided that she hated when she had to wait for me to finish with the patient who preceded her on Wednesday afternoons.

"He looks like such an awful bore," she said, and when I did not respond, she blurted, "I can take it that you have your own family, but other patients? It seems so . . . I don't know, so *promiscuous!*"

I could read the writing on the wall: Mary was in danger of slipping from positive transference into an intractable negative transference. In this process I would remain the object of her displaced feelings for her father, but negative feelings would dominate to the virtual exclusion of all other feelings; the hurt, anger, and resentment that she felt toward her real father would be directed at me, her substitute father, and none of the positive feelings she felt toward me would survive. I was at risk of becoming Mary's "bad parent," with the attendant distrust of that parent. It was a time for me to proceed with extreme caution. It was also time to begin helping Mary work toward her independence of me.

So in February I decided to begin preparing Mary for the

summer break in our therapy. This interruption can be a problem for patients in general but, I am afraid, more of a problem for my patients because I take *two* full months away from my practice every summer instead of the customary one month. My whole family retires to a rather primitive "camp" on Lake Champlain for the months of July and August so that we can reconnect with one another and get back in touch with something deeper in ourselves, something that requires long days deep in uncultivated nature without any schedule. I have always told myself that this respite makes me a better therapist, a better conduit of the life-force. But of course, I know that it is mostly selfishness that propels me out of New York for those two months every summer.

Mary instantly became sullen when I told her.

"But I will always be available to you for phone calls—*long* phone sessions—whenever you feel the need," I assured her.

"What is this we do here, some kind of a hobby of yours?" she blurted. It was the first sarcasm I had heard come out of her mouth.

"Taking a long vacation does not mean that I am not devoted to my work," I said, defensive in spite of myself.

Toward the end of that February session Mary abruptly looked at me and said, "So, have you changed your mind yet?"

"About what?"

"This summer."

"No, Mary. Why would I change my mind now?"

Mary shook her head. "I should have known," she muttered. "This is all just an illusion."

"What is an illusion?" I asked.

"You know," she replied. "All of this. Everything that goes on in here."

That was it. Mary turned icy cold in front of my eyes, and in the following ten weeks she completely withdrew from me. My attempt at caution had backfired on me.

Late in the afternoon of the Monday of the break-in I received a call from Rolf Griswold's attorney, a Mr. Richard Brentwood. He said that he would like to see a copy of Beverly Griswold's records so that he could have a psychiatrist of his own choosing evaluate her fitness as a mother. I informed Mr. Brentwood that those records were confidential.

"Do you intend to testify at the custody hearing on Mrs. Griswold's behalf?" the lawyer demanded.

"If she asks me to, yes," I answered.

"Then I have the right to inspect your records—full disclosure, so that when I cross-examine—"

"Good-bye, Mr. Brentwood," I said.

"Look, if you don't want to give them to me, I'll just subpoena them," the lawyer said. "I'm going to get them one way or another."

"What's the matter, Brentwood?" I said, raising my voice. "Couldn't Rolf find what he wanted last night?"

"What the hell are you talking about?"

"Ask your client," I said, and hung up.

That night after dinner I returned to my office and went through all of my records. Fortunately I have them page-numbered and coded so it is not difficult to determine if any pages are missing. I paid particular attention to Beverly Griswold's file. There were smudges on several of the pages—from cigarette ashes, I guessed—but nothing was missing from this or any other file. In fact, the only item I could not put my hands on was a small onyx jaguar that a friend had bought for me in Mexico.

I had purchased a new bolt lock, and at around eleven o'clock I went to work replacing the old lock with the new. The phone in my office started ringing.

"Hello?"

Nothing.

"Who is this?"

Nothing.

"Listen, you must want something. And you can't get it if you don't talk to me."

Still nothing.

"In case you didn't know, breaking and entering is a felony. I wouldn't try that again if I were you."

The phone went dead.

As I set my phone back into its cradle, I saw that my hand was trembling. *Damn him! Damn him, whoever it was!* I was finally feeling the full impact of my vulnerability. I had been holding back my anger all day while I saw my patients, but now I was shaking with fury. The idea of calling the police suddenly seemed quite reasonable. Who the hell was I protecting anyhow? What if I simply asked them to rig my phone to trace my secret caller? It might end up being for my tormentor's own good. Whoever it was obviously was in need of help.

Tuesday morning I set off down the hallway at quarter to eight to see my first patient of the day, Jack Noto. With no patient preceding him and a buffer of ten minutes before the patient after him arrived, Jack was guaranteed total privacy from my other patients, although it always seemed to me that being seen by my other patients was the least of his worries.

Jack was waiting for me outside my office door with a look of utter desolation on his face.

"How's it going, Jack?" I said as I let us both in.

"Shitty." He groaned. "My life is pure, unadulterated shit."

It was Jack's standard opener.

Less than four years earlier Jack had been a Wall Street lawyer specializing in international banking. He had arrived at this position via the fast track from Yale College and Georgetown Law School. Married to his college sweetheart, Jack owned a sports car, an apartment on Gramercy Park, and a second home on Fire Island, all by the time he was twenty-nine years old. And then he started taking dope. He had been turned on to cocaine by business associates in Brazil and Argentina. At the time it was considered chic on the Street to snort a line or two during coffee breaks. It sharpened the reflexes, made a man more competitive, helped the day sail by faster. Or so it seemed to Jack Noto.

His colleagues at his law firm saw things differently; they found Jack increasingly erratic and unreliable. They called him on bad judgments a few times, then finally let him go. Jack had a "nut" of close to ten thousand dollars a month what with his various mortgages and maintenance costs, not to mention his drug habit, so he turned naturally to a business that paid even more than corporate lawyering: cocaine dealing. In less than a year he became one of the key players in the metropolitan area, with a decidedly upscale clientele: entertainers, producers, business executives.

Gayle, Jack's wife, hated what had happened to her husband. She was pregnant and kept saying, "What are you going to tell our son when he asks you what you do for a living?" She told Jack that unless he got out of the business before the child was born, she was going to leave him. It was not an idle threat. Jack told her to trust him, that he was going to get out, but that it wasn't that easy. He had a number of loose ends that needed tidying up.

Jack's major loose end was the three hundred thousand dollars he owed his supplier in Buenos Aires, money Jack had used to buy a boat for one of his couriers. Jack asked his supplier to be patient, but like his wife, Jack's supplier gave him a deadline. This was not an idle threat either.

It was at this point that Jack decided he needed psychological help. By the time he came to see to me, he had been turned down by four therapists, all of whom had declared that they could not in good conscience treat a criminal. I, on the other hand, could not in good conscience *refuse* to treat a criminal who said that he desperately wanted help going straight.

My conditions for working with Jack were simple: First, he had to join Narcotics Anonymous and begin to kick his own cocaine habit; second, he could not tell anybody that he was seeing me.

"I've been getting very sloppy in my work," Jack told me at that first session. "Making calls from my home phone, late for drops, all the basic no-nos of the trade. Actually I think I have an unconscious need to get caught."

Only a dope dealer with a Yale education would come up with that bit of self-analysis. But we did not have time for psychoanalysis. Jack needed some quick behavior modification along with some radical career counseling. I began immediately by taking Jack on guided fantasy trips:

"Imagine you are driving your car. Gayle's in the front seat. She's eight months pregnant by now. And there's this car following you. You can see it in the rearview mirror. Do you see the car, Jack?"

"Yes."

"There are four men in that car. You recognize one of them. You met him in Buenos Aires. They pull alongside you. Their guns are pointed out the window at you. They force you to stop. And then they pull open the side door and yank out Gayle."

"Okay, enough, I get the idea, Doctor."

"Stick with it, Jack. We aren't done yet. Your friend from Buenos Aires pulls out a knife and pushes it up against Gayle's throat. He says he wants to know where his money is."

The point of these guided fantasies was to put Jack back in touch with reality. His two years on drugs had dulled his sense of cause and effect.

I have to admit to enjoying my sessions with Jack. His life had a seductive edge to it, and our goal was clear-cut, if not particularly easy to achieve. But as of the break-in to my office, my interest in Jack's "edge" had diminished significantly. That event had provided *me* with a sense of reality that had somehow eluded me.

On this Tuesday morning Jack had more bad news to tell me. Gayle had moved out two days ago. A drug dealer named

Carlos had put Jack on notice that he was taking over his Broadway clients. And the man from Buenos Aires had called to say that Jack had only ten days left to pay his debt.

"Well, at least you don't have any more decisions to make," I said to Jack. "Time to pay the piper."

"With what, exactly?"

"Sell everything you've got, Jack. Your apartment, your furniture, your house, your car. Sell it all, pay your debts, and start over clean. You don't have any other options left, get it?"

Jack nodded his head, then looked directly at me.

"Listen, are you okay, Akeret?" he asked abruptly.

"Yes, fine. Why?"

"Remember when I phoned you last week?" Jack said.

"Yes."

"It was from my home phone. And it turns out it's been bugged. Not by the police, by Carlos, the guy who's trying to take over my territory. I'm afraid he now knows who you are and what I do in here."

I paused a moment.

"Just get out of the business, Jack. Right now, okay?" I said. It hardly seemed the right time to be burdening him with my own fears. I did not mention the break-in.


MY DAUGHTERS have always liked to have a hand in decorating my waiting room. They drew pictures in school and hung them on the walls; my eldest made a felt valentine that she attached to the inside of the door; my youngest, Teal, dried some wild flowers from Lake Champlain and arranged them in a vase on the coffee table.

The Monday after the break-in, when I opened my office door to let Mary McGinely in, I saw that there was a bouquet of fresh tulips in that vase and that the stems of the dried flowers were now obtruding from the wastebasket. Mary watched me take this in.

"It's spring, eh, Doctor?" she said gaily. "I thought this place could use a little cheering up."

I did not reply. I recalled that some months earlier Mary had asked me where I had gotten the dried flowers and I'd told her that they were a gift from Teal.

Once we were inside my office, Mary reverted to icy silence. I waited. Nothing. I thanked her for the flowers. She shrugged. I told her for what must have been the fiftieth time that by just sitting there revealing nothing of what she was feeling, she was wasting a valuable opportunity to learn about herself. She was unimpressed. And then, probably in allergic reaction to the tulips, I coughed. It was one of those self-perpetuating coughs that tickle the back of the throat, making me need to cough again. In the midst of my little fit, I caught a glimpse of Mary staring at me. Her face was crimson, her mouth had dropped open, and her eyes were wet. She looked frightened.

I had little idea of what to make of Mary's highly charged reaction, but I did know that it provided us with a rare opportunity to reach down into her well of unexpressed emotions.

"Tell me about your father," I said urgently. "Any memory. Anything at all. Right now."

I could literally see a memory rising to the surface of Mary's broad face, see tears forming in the corners of her eyes, and then I saw her start to squeeze that memory back down.

"Don't think about it. Just say it!" I said, leaning toward her.

"It—it's late at night," she stammered in a monotone, her eyes closed. "I can't sleep. I don't know why. I'm just tossing and turning. So I go downstairs, and there are Mother and Father watching television. A late movie. Mother gives me a severe look, like 'What are you doing up at this hour?' But Father, he—he just waves me over and lifts me up onto his lap. Doesn't look at me especially. Just keeps looking at the movie with me cradled in his lap. And I—I—I feel so unbelievably good. So—so—"

Mary was fighting back her tears so strenuously that she had to stop.

"Let it go," I said softly.

Mary shook her head.

"Go ahead. Let it go," I repeated.

"No!"

"Why not, Mary?"

"Because—because if I start crying, I'll never stop!" she blurted.

"No, you won't. You'll stop when you're finished," I assured her.

"But what if I don't?" Mary snapped angrily. "What if it gets to be July and I'm still crying? Huh? What then? Will you stay here until I'm finished crying?"

"All right," I said, smiling. "If you cry straight through to July, I *will* stay here."

But Mary was not amused. She looked me fiercely in the eye and said, "You just like to make people suffer by getting close and then leaving them."

"Who else does that remind you of?" I asked.

"Nobody else! *Just you!*" Mary exploded.

And that is all she said for the rest of that session.

Later that same day Beverly Griswold came in for her hour. For several weeks now it had been my pleasure to see her looking stronger and more confident.

When Beverly first came for help four months earlier, she had arrived at my door with a swollen face, a black eye, and a line of fresh stitches across her forehead, the result of her most recent beating by her husband, Rolf, an alcoholic with a Jekyll and Hyde personality. When drunk, Rolf was extremely cruel and violent. He would accuse her of being unfaithful to him (she was not), would beat her and threaten to kill her. Beverly knew that she had to leave him, but she was afraid to—afraid of what he might do to her and to their twin sons, afraid that somehow she was to blame for the failure of her marriage. That was Rolf's line, that Beverly had sabotaged their marriage from the start, that it was she who drove him to violence.

I told her that it was irrelevant to try to assign blame at this point in their relationship. First she had to secure her and her sons' safety. Then she and her husband could try to work things out in neutral territory, preferably a therapist's office. With my encouragement, Beverly separated from Rolf and obtained a restraining order to keep him away from her apartment. She then asked him to go into couple therapy with her, but Rolf refused. She was the sick one, Rolf insisted. And so, finally, Beverly had filed for divorce, seeking full-time custody of the children.

Today she told me that the custody hearing had been scheduled for next week. She said her lawyer wanted me to testify on her psychological fitness in court. I told her about my call from Rolf's lawyer.

"Let him have my records if he wants them," Beverly said. "I have nothing to be ashamed of—do I?"

"Not a thing," I said. "But it's a matter of principle with me. Nobody sees my records."

"You're the doctor," she replied, smiling happily.

That night I received another of my mute phone calls.

"Speak up, Rolf, I can't hear you!" I shouted into the phone. No response.

"Is that you, Carlos? Listen, I don't have what you're looking for! You hear? So forget it, will you?"

I slammed down the phone. I was trembling uncontrollably. God help me, this was getting to me.

The events of the next few days did little to allay my anxiety. Thursday I discovered that my fountain pen was missing from my office desk. Friday morning a server arrived at my door with a subpoena for Beverly Griswold's records. I refused to let him in. And Sunday evening my daughter Teal returned home from taking our dog for a walk in Riverside Park looking shaken.

"Somebody was following me," she said.

"Are you sure?"

"Yes," Teal said.

"What did he look like?" I asked her.

"It wasn't a he," Teal said. "It was a lady. Big. Pretty. With sad blue eyes."

DRIVING NORTH on California's coastal Highway 1, I entered redwood country with Phil Ochs crooning on my tape player:

. . . A race around the stars, a journey through the Universe ablaze with changes. . . .

On my right a sign announced the turnoff to Big Sur, home in the sixties and seventies to the Esalen Institute, the very last word in experimental psychotherapies. I wondered if Esalen was still there and, if so, what it was up to now.

Psychotherapy started going wild and crazy back in the sixties. Many of my colleagues began seeing themselves not simply as healers of the individual but as prime agents of a social revolution. The times were achanging, and some therapists believed they had a unique historic obligation to bust the whole culture out of a prison of emotional and sexual repression—and to do it fast.

To reach this extraordinary goal, extraordinary means were required, and the subtle, slow-moving, brainy techniques of classical psychoanalysis did not seem up to the task. Many therapists turned to the radical ideas of Wilhelm Reich, author of *The Sexual Revolution* (he coined that phrase), a man who had once been a member of Vienna's inner circle of Freudians, but who ended his days in 1957 in an federal American prison, scorned by the psychiatric establishment for his heresies. Now Reich's ideas were being resurrected and repackaged as Gestalt therapy, bioenergetics, and Rolfing, to name just a few of the novel therapies that began to flourish then. To liberate a person from the socioreligious straitjacket of Western civilization, these therapies used touch (including painful deep tissue massage), psychodrama, nudity, scream fests, regression games, LSD trips—whatever could put a person through rapid and radical "changes."

Inevitably some of that spirit of therapeutic invention and adventure slipped through the door of my own office. It appealed to that part of me, already nurtured by Fromm, that believed that people do not change by words alone. It had always seemed obvious to me that there was all the difference in the world between someone's saying, "I feel angry," and someone's actually *feeling* his anger, *acting* it out, and *reexperiencing* it.

I started experimenting in my therapy groups. What if, instead of just talking, we got out of our chairs, walked around, touched one another, acted out our fantasies? What would happen if we could regress for an hour, become the children we once were instead of merely recalling our childhoods? What if we played the part of our own parents to see what that felt like? What if, instead of simply recalling and recounting our dreams, we acted them out, too? What if, for one entire group session, words were forbidden? With what feelings would these experiences put us in touch? And would contacting those feelings really help us to change in any fundamental way?

We pressed our imaginations. We acted like fools. We frightened ourselves. We laughed hysterically. And every once in a long while something would happen that would propel one of us into a whole new realm of feeling and perception.

I WAITED UNTIL ten past nine before I started coughing. It was the Monday morning after the Sunday evening when my daughter Teal had returned from the park shaken. Mary was sitting across from me, withdrawn, cold, immobile. I coughed the way I had the last time, a dry, hacking cough that would seem just about to stop when it would start all over again, louder, more violent. I coughed so hard that I could feel my face turning red, my eyes smarting. I coughed harder and harder and then suddenly reached with both my hands to the left side of my chest, grimaced anguishedly, and cried out, "My heart! My heart!" Then I slumped down in my chair, letting my mouth drop open as if I were dead.

Silence. I could feel my heart thudding in my chest from the exertion of it all.

Then Mary's wail. An awful, mournful wail that seemed to come from a great distance. It did. It came from across twenty years.

"Oh, God! I didn't mean it! Please! Please! *I swear I didn't mean it!*"

I held my breath. I did not move.

Mary started to cry hysterically, choking, sputtering, gasping for air, now wailing, "No! No! *Not again!*"

Listening to that terrible keening sound, I could indeed imagine it going on forever. She cried this way for several minutes, then finally slowed to a stuttering whimper. My eyes were closed, but now I could hear her getting out of her chair and slowly approaching me. She reached out, grasped my face in both her hands. I was sure that she was about to start giving me mouth-to-mouth resuscitation. It was time for me to bring my act to an end, to break the spell. I opened my eyes and looked up at her.

"I'm okay," I whispered.

I expected Mary to be furious with me—from her point of view, I surely deserved it—but looking into her sad blue eyes, I saw that she remained in the thrall of a more profound emotion. She still had her palms pressed against my cheeks, her tortured face hovering just above mine.

"What did you think you'd done to me?" I asked softly.

"Killed you. I was sure I'd killed you," she answered, still whimpering.

"How? How had you killed me?"

"By wishing you dead," Mary answered. "By murdering you in my heart."

I did not have to ask why she wanted me dead; she had already told me that: *You just like to make people suffer by getting close and then leaving them.*

"The same way you wished your father dead?" I said.

Mary abruptly pulled her hands away from my cheeks. Her own face had drained pale.

"Why did you say that?" she said in a monotone.

"Most children wish their parents dead at one time or another. And perhaps you had more reason than most. Your father wasn't there for you. He hurt you—more than he realized."

Mary winced when I said this.

"But not many fathers actually die on cue." I went on. "Exactly when you wish him dead. Yours did, didn't he?"

Mary backed to her chair and sat down without taking her eyes off mine.

"I've never told this to a soul," she said in a half whisper. "Not even to the fathers. I couldn't."

She closed her eyes. I waited.

"I was around eight the first time." She began. "He had a meeting in town, in Hartford, at the home office. And I had to bring him some papers that he'd left at the house. When I came up to the office, he introduced me to his boss, and his boss said, 'Gee, Harry, I didn't know you had a daughter named Mary. I've got a Mary, too, you know.' I could have died right there on the spot. Father hadn't even mentioned me. It was like I didn't exist. And I remember thinking, If I don't exist, I wish you didn't exist either. I wish you were dead!"

"But he didn't die then," I said.

"No, he didn't die, but he did get sick. Pneumonia. He was in the hospital for two weeks," Mary said.

"You'd wished him there," I said.

Mary nodded, silent for a moment before going on.

"Two years later I was at St. Elizabeth's School. Father was home, in the living room, watching a Notre Dame football game. And I wanted to show him my report card. I'd gotten three As and two Bs. I was so excited that I tripped on the coffee table and knocked over his beer. He blew up at me and I started to cry and he said, 'If you don't shut up, I'll really give you something to cry about.' And that's when I said it, yelled it right at him: 'I wish you were dead!' " Mary took a deep breath. "They took him to the hospital that night. He was dead the next day."

"And you really think that you killed him, don't you?" I said.

"Yes."

"It doesn't work that way, you know. Wishes aren't that powerful. They can't influence events all by themselves."

"You don't know that for sure," Mary retorted.

"Of course I do. Wishes don't come true very often at all. Mine don't, that's for sure," I replied.

"That's because you don't have the power," Mary said.

"Maybe you don't either," I said. "If you did, I would have been dead long ago. Say, about the time I told you I was going away for two months."

Mary had started whimpering again.

"I—I didn't *really* wish you were dead," she stammered.

"Sure, you did. You did and you didn't. Both wishes." I hesitated a moment, then added, "Just like you did with my daughter Teal."

"No! No!" Mary looked terrified. "I just—I just—"

And then she started crying in earnest again. I waited for several minutes. More was coming, I could tell.

"That—that was me," Mary stammered finally. "On the

phone. I had to call, to see if you were still alive. To see if I'd actually—"

"I know," I said softly.

I had finally figured that out when Teal described her shadow to me the night before. Then it had all become clear to me, all the connections: Mary's denial of feelings about her father's death, her belief in the lethal power of her wishes, the parity of guilt for wishes with guilt for actions in her Catholic training. Then there was Mary's fury at me for my plans to go away for two months, her inability to express that fury fully, and finally her attempt to "replace" Teal by replacing Teal's flowers with her own—perhaps so she could replace Teal altogether in my family.

I suppose I should have put this all together sooner than that evening. But I had these other, so much more promising suspects.

"You don't know who I am, not really." Mary went on. "You don't know how bad I really am."

I was pretty certain what was coming next.

"I have your pen," she said. "I stole it off your desk. And I have your little jaguar, too."

I nodded, waiting for the final revelation: the break-in. But Mary just sat there, gazing at me apprehensively, and nothing more came. Was confession over?

"When? When did you take the pen?" I asked.

"I don't know. When you weren't looking. At the end of a session. I just grabbed it. Same with the jaguar," Mary said.

I smiled. No, it wasn't Mary who had broken into my office; she certainly would have confessed to that now if she had. But another, far more important mystery had been solved this morning.

"*Why aren't you angry at me?*" Mary suddenly bellowed at me.

"Because now we can finally get down to work," I said.

Mary and I worked together for another two years, but that was the morning that we turned the corner. After that childhood memories came gushing out of her. She recalled how she had gone through most of her childhood squinting in what appeared to the other children like a perpetual grimace, until it was finally discovered that she needed glasses; she remembered her humiliation when she was the only girl in her class not to be invited to the grammar school tea dance; and she recalled one slight after another from her preoccupied parents, including their failure even to attend her confirmation. During these years we explored what the issues of being a "good girl" and a "bad girl" had to do with being a "real" grown woman. We talked about her need to be loved "specially" and unconditionally and the ways in which that love could and could not be available to her now as a wife. And we talked about the hole in her life that would never completely be filled because she would never have the father she needed when she was young.

I believe the occasional end-of-therapy session hug was worth a thousand spoken words.

When we finally said good-bye in 1977, Mary was fully committed to her marriage, two months pregnant, and very independent and happy.

I did not testify at the custody hearing for Beverly Griswold's children, but I was permitted to submit to the court a written summary of Beverly's case in which I described her as a fine, loving mother and Rolf as an abusive husband and potentially dangerous father. Beverly was awarded full custody of the twins as well as a generous alimony. Rolf disappeared without paying a cent.

Jack Noto not only got out of the drug business but managed to get out with a profit: He struck a cash deal with Carlos for personal introductions to all his customers. Jack was by then free of his own drug dependency. He moved to Virginia

Beach, where he opened a successful seafood restaurant. He wrote me from there informing me that he and his wife had reconciled; she had given birth to a daughter, and they were currently expecting a second child.

I never found out who broke into my office.

MARY ASKED ME to meet her at her workplace, the North County Parent / Child Center in Eureka, California. The center is housed in a brown-shingle cottage tangled with violet bougainvillaea, making it look like an illustration in a nursery book. When I gave my name to the receptionist, a fresh-faced Latina woman, she smiled broadly.

"He's here, Mary!" she called down the corridor, then turned back to me and said, "We hear about you all the time. Every day it's Dr. Akeret would say this, Dr. Akeret would approach it this way. I feel like I know you already."

"Sounds like you have good reason to resent me already, too," I said, grinning.

"Not at all," the woman replied. "Mary is a saint. And from what she tells us, she owes everything to you."

I smiled uncomfortably. Then, from the corner of my eye, I saw Mary walking toward me, her face beaming.

"Robi!" She threw her arms around me, planted a big kiss on each of my cheeks.

"Hello, Mary. You look terrific."

She did, indeed, look very good. Although still plump, even plumper than seventeen years ago, Mary had the smooth-skinned, ruddy face of a college girl. Her gray-streaked blond hair hung loose to her shoulders, her pale blue eyes were bright and warm, and her wide-open smile seemed to broadcast that this was a woman who took pleasure in her life.

"Let me show you around," she said, putting her arm through mine.

She led me from one room to another: a day-care nursery, a teen pregnancy support group, a class in healthy eating on a low budget. The moment we entered each room, the leader would stop what she was doing and greet me like an old friend. They had all heard about me; they were honored to meet me finally. I found myself blushing with a mix of pride and vague unease.

But there was nothing ambiguous about my reaction to the North County Parent / Child Center: I was deeply impressed by it. The center boasted the lowest teen pregnancy rate in Northern California, a relatively high birth weight among its clients' babies, along with a low incidence of infant mortality, child abuse, and other family violence. And, everyone said, it was all thanks to Mary McGinely, the center's founding director.

Mary had arranged it so that we could drive together in my van back to her house, a good three-quarters of an hour away. The first thing I said to her as we started off was how impressed I was with the center and her leadership there. Mary smiled proudly.

"It's a dream job," she said, then laughed. "I get to be a nun without the habit. What's more, I still get to sleep with my husband."

As we drove along the inland road, Mary caught me up on the past seventeen years of her life. It was, for the most part, one happy story after another.

She gave birth to her son, Jared, in 1977, and he'd now grown into a bright, handsome, and gregarious young man with a good heart and strong ambitions. She and her husband, Mal, were immensely proud of him.

"One of the wonderful things about life is that you really do get a second chance to 'get it right,' and that's with your children," Mary said. "Neither Mal nor I had the best of childhoods, but now we get to do all the things for Jared and Gloria [their daughter] that we missed in our own lives. And it kind of works retroactively: By nurturing them, we nurture that part of ourselves that still needs it."

Mal's career in folk music had had its ups and downs. One recording of original songs had done quite well, but a second one had not, mostly, she thought, because of a general waning of interest in the form. But Mal almost always had a "money" job of one kind or another—currently he was a school bus driver—and he continued to take pleasure in his music. For the most part, Mary said, she and Mal had become closer over the years, more tolerant of each other, more loving, more intimate. They both reveled in family life, just the simple daily events of eating dinner together, going to Jared's high school basketball games (he was a starting guard), attending church together.

"Yes, I finally went back," Mary said, winking. "You never stray from the church for long, you know. It's like prison; it always draws you back."

She giggled like a schoolgirl.

"Just kidding, Robi," she said. "Actually I became an Episcopalian, which is sort of Catholicism with the guilt filtered out. But the ritual is still there, and it still resonates for me. And of course, the basic stuff, the loving-thy-neighbor stuff, is what gives me the most pleasure in my life."

She went on to tell me that she had developed a close relationship with the priest in her local Episcopal parish, a man named Wesley Galk. In time she had become director of his Sunday school and helped him set up various church outreach programs for the poor and elderly. But after several years Galk had suddenly departed to become rector of a church in San Francisco.

"He left me high and dry," Mary said dolefully. "One day we're making plans to start a meals-on-wheels program; the next day he's out of here. It kind of hurt."

The road narrowed as it spun through the hills north of Eureka. Mary's story about Wesley Galk had a familiar ring to it, but I did not comment on that. We drove in silence for a few minutes. Then Mary began to tell me about her own career.

Not long after Jared was born, she had gone back to graduate school and taken degrees in advanced nursing and clinic management. A paper she wrote in school led to a job writing a "pocket" medical dictionary and a general nursing reference catalog, the royalties from which had allowed her to buy their house in Korbel. For many years she had divided her time among midwifery, private home nursing, and teaching at a local junior college, but five years ago the opportunity to start the North County Parent / Child Center had arisen, and since then she has devoted full-time to it.

"The center has gotten all kinds of recognition," she told me. "Plaques from the governor, write-ups in the papers. In some areas of community care we've kind of set the standard for the rest of the state."

I again told Mary how proud I was of her achievement, and she patted the back of my hand in appreciation.

During all these years Mal and Mary had tried without success to have another child. Then, one year after Mary started the center, a foster child of three who appeared in the center's nursery turned out to need a new home. That child was Gloria. Mal and Mary adopted her as soon as they could, and she has been a member of the family ever since.

"The whole business has not been without its problems," Mary told me. "There were signs that Gloria suffered some pretty horrendous abuse and neglect before we got her. At one point Gloria and I went into therapy together to try to work through some of that stuff. But of course, the only real cure is years and years of hugs. A thousand hugs for every slap that child endured. A thousand hugs for every time she was left alone in a locked room."

Mary abruptly smiled. "We do an awful lot of hugging in our house," she said. "Jared's finally reached the age where he's getting a little sick of it. He says he's trying to kick the habit, going to join Huggers Anonymous."

I laughed along with her. Mary rolled open her window and let the evening air blow against her face.

"I'm so happy to see you!" she cried. "I do love you, you know. We all do in my family. We're grateful, you see."

I could not think of what to say in reply. That vague unease had returned again.

"I haven't told you about Billy Donahue, have I?" Mary said cheerily, hurrying us by that awkward moment.

"No, who's that?"

"My father's best friend from high school."

Mary proceeded to tell me how she had connected with Donahue. It seems Mary's mother had received a letter from an agency that traces graduates for high school reunion committees. Her mother had written back informing them that her husband had passed away some twenty-odd years ago, but when she mentioned the letter to Mary, Mary had written to the reunion people saying that she would be interested in meeting her father's old friends. Next thing she knew, she was flying east to have dinner with Billy Donahue and his family in New Haven.

"We hit it off right away," Mary told me. "Billy told me hundreds of stories about him and Dad in school, on the football team, dating girls, everything. It was the first time Dad really came alive for me, and guess what? I liked him. Liked what I heard about him.

"So Billy and I began this wonderful correspondence. He and his wife visited us out here a couple times. We sent each other Christmas presents and birthday presents. Right up until Billy died two years ago."

That story again. But again I did not comment.

"Hey! I know what you're thinking, Robi," Mary said cheerfully. " 'She's still looking for a father. First it's Wesley Galk; then it's Billy Donahue. She's still got a daddy hang-up.' Am I right?"

"Something like that," I said, smiling back.

"Well, the difference is that now I'm conscious of what I'm doing," Mary said. "And it turns out there are a lot of women out there just like me. I keep a journal that's devoted just to that subject. Quotes and things. My favorite quote is from Nancy Friday: 'For those of us who did not have a father, teachers and leaders are irresistible.' That about sums it up, doesn't it?"

We were now in Korbel, and Mary directed me to her house, a one-story cottage with broken shingles in a relatively poor section of town. I pulled up in the driveway behind the family pickup truck and was reaching for my door handle when Mary touched my hand.

"There's one thing I've got to say, Robi, and I'd like to say it now." She began in a hushed voice. "It's this theory of mine. You see, everybody has an influence on everybody else, but some have more than others. Like parents and priests and therapists and nurses. Well, you had an incredible influence on me, and now it seems I'm having it on other people—on the mothers and families I work with. So it's kind of a spreading thing. Mal calls it my Trickle-down Theory of Goodness. He says it's the only kind of trickle-down economics that's ever going to have anything to do with us."

"Thank you," I said.

"You're welcome, Robi," Mary said, and she planted another kiss on my cheek.

Mal, Jared, and Gloria were waiting for us in the kitchen with a splendid dinner that they had been working on all afternoon: a roasted chicken, mashed potatoes, string beans with almonds, cranberry sauce, and a boat of thick, creamy gravy. It was a relaxed, joking family that reminded me of my own when my girls were still at home. The entire family peppered me with questions about the different parts of the country I'd visited. The only serious question came from young Jared, who had heard about the purpose of my trip.

"So, what's the verdict?" he asked me. "Does therapy work?"

I noticed that Mary was regarding me soberly.

"You got me," I said, smiling at the boy. "All the evidence isn't in yet."

"It works all right!" Mary chimed.

"Maybe it only works when it works," Mal said.

"You said a mouthful," I said.

"Yeah, he always talks with his mouth full," Gloria said, and we all laughed.

After dinner Mal took out his guitar right at the kitchen table and sang a couple of songs he'd written recently. I found one particularly enchanting, a wry and tender folk ballad that he called "Family Man." Mary had seen my guitar case in the van and now urged me to bring it in. It didn't take much coaxing. Mal and I sang a few old Phil Ochs and Bob Dylan songs together. It was a wonderful evening, and when Mary walked with me to the van to say good night, I thanked her for it. It was difficult to be certain in the moonlight, but I thought I saw her blush.

After several days of sampling the motels of the Southwest, I had decided to treat myself to a bed-and-breakfast that Mary recommended, the Korbel Inn. The owners gave me a large room overlooking a starry pasture. I took a long shower and lay down on top of the double bed in my robe. That feeling of malaise had come back again; in fact, it seemed that it had never completely left me all day.

Did I doubt that Mary was as happy, strong, and well adjusted as she presented herself to me?

Not really. Everything about her seemed so spontaneous and unfiltered: her laughter, her kisses, her declarations of pride in her work, her expressions of gratitude for all that had been given her. I did not sense one false gesture, one mediated response. So what was bothering me?

The pattern of her relentless search for a substitute father? That certainly smacked of unfinished emotional business. But Mary had insisted that *being conscious* of her lifelong longing

for a father made all the difference in the world, removed it
from the realm of neurotic compulsions. That longing was, she
said, a fundamental fact of her life, and facts of life don't just
go away; all you can do is become conscious of them and learn
to live with them. That is exactly what I believe, too.

Was it Mary's strong attachment to me that made me so
uneasy? That and her undying gratitude?

That got closer to it, I think. Especially all that gratitude.
The phrase that kept popping in my mind was "Too good to
be true."

But what was that about? Was the Therapist suddenly
turning modest and bashful? *Aw, shucks, ma'am, I didn't really
do anything.*

What, after all, was the goal of this entire cross-country
odyssey of mine? Certainly the underlying dream that set it in
motion was to have a happy, well-adjusted former patient of
mine say, earnestly, "Thank you, Doctor. You changed my
life."

Wasn't it?

Or did I, too, have to be wary of what I desired?

Mary met me at the inn for a leisurely breakfast the next
morning. We mostly talked about her work. She was taking
some courses in pastoral counseling that sounded quite interesting to me.

"In one of my classes we're discussing fear of closeness, and
I couldn't help but think how before our work, I never got close
to anyone, knowing only separation and loss would follow.
What I learned with you was that it's okay to get close, to
risk losing someone and the pain it entails, because it's the
connection, not the fear of losing it, that matters most."

That, I reminded myself, is well worth all those endless
silent negative hours we endured during the long haul of our
therapy.

At around ten I noticed her check her watch a couple of

times. I asked if they were expecting her at the center, and reluctantly she said yes. I told her that I had to be leaving soon myself. I walked her out to her truck.

"You know, there's something I've been dying to ask you since you arrived, Robi," she said abruptly. "Do you remember those awful phantom phone calls I made to you?"

"How could I forget them?"

"Well, I never told you this, but you really worried me. You sounded so angry. You thought I was somebody named Carlos one time. And somebody named Rolf another. Who were they anyway?"

I burst out laughing and then told her.


Mary teared up when we said good-bye.

I was on my way home, where I would stop a day or two before I left for my final destination, Paris. I found myself eager to get to New York as soon as possible. For the first time since I set out on my journey, I was starting to feel a bit homesick. I had had enough of being the Lone Ranger.

Somewhere in Idaho I phoned Ann from a motel room. She told me that she had received a call from Mary McGinely just a few hours earlier and that Mary had sounded distraught. Mary wanted me to get in touch with her immediately.

I waited several minutes after hanging up with Ann before I phoned Korbel. This had been a mistake, I told myself again. A huge mistake, all of it. I had no right to reinsert myself into my former patients' lives, even if they were willing to have me there. Why hadn't I realized that before I started all of this?

"Hello?"

"Mary? It's Robi—Dr. Akeret."

"Oh, God, Robi, I'm sorry! I'm—I'm terribly sorry!" Mary stammered.

"Sorry for what? What's the problem, Mary?"

"Sorry for stealing from you."

"That was a long time ago, Mary. That's all over."

"No, your guitar pick. I stole it out of your case when you were here," Mary said.

I stared at the phone, dumbfounded. My guitar pick?

"All those years," Mary said. "All those years, and I still have the same problem."

Suddenly a laugh escaped from my throat. I started to cover the phone lest Mary hear it but decided not to. No, let her hear it!

"What are you laughing at?" she snapped angrily.

"You!" I said. "St. Mary!"

"I am not St. Mary!" she cried.

"No, you're not, are you?" I said. "And thank God for that! I was starting to think you were absolutely perfect, and it was giving me the creeps."

"What are you talking about?"

"The good girl rides again, now in California," I said. "I found it a little hard to take. Too good to be true."

"But I really am happy," Mary protested. "My work, my family. That's all true, Robi."

"I know it is. It's just not perfect, that's all. And it doesn't have to be. Not for me, not for you. That's what your little theft was about, I think. It was letting us both know that. It was letting us both off the hook."

"Both of us?" Mary asked.

"Yes," I said. "I wasn't exactly comfortable being St. Robi either."

We must have talked on the phone for a good hour and a half that night. I don't think I learned anything radically new about her life, no big confessions, but the tone of our conversation had changed from the too-good-to-be-trueness of the day I had spent with her to something much more real. It's a lot easier to make human contact when nobody is a saint.

Just before falling asleep that night, I remembered a story that I once heard the gifted analyst Frieda Fromm-Reichmann tell. It was about a patient who always picked the skin off her feet until they bled. As therapy progressed, this patient changed dramatically, yet she continued to pick savagely at her feet right up to their last session. When Dr. Fromm-Reichmann asked why, after all her progress, she persisted in this self-destructive habit, the patient replied, "It reminds me of where I've been."

I slept better that night than I had in days. The malaise was gone.

# FIVE

# Sasha: The Beast

Narcissism, the fairy tale ["Beauty and the Beast"]
teaches, despite its seeming attractiveness, is not a life
of satisfactions, but no life at all.

Bruno Bettelheim, *The Uses of Enchantment*

SITTING IN A SIDEWALK CAFÉ in St.-Germain-des-
Prés, I cannot escape the idea that even the subtlest variations of our notion of normality are culturally deter-
mined. Next to me, a Frenchman in his seventies wearing a
silk shirt and a brightly colored foulard blatantly ogles a leggy
woman half his age as she strolls by in a miniskirt.

Is this piggish behavior the result of overcompensation for
the inevitable fears of impotency that aging brings with it?

The young woman turns her finely modeled head toward
the man and smiles enchantingly. Not a word is spoken, but as
their eyes meet, the communication between them is quite
clear: She is thanking him for his acknowledgment of her sexual attractiveness; he is thanking her for her generosity in
sharing her beauty. There are no expectations on either part
beyond this little exchange.

Sexual harassment? Symptoms of sexual insecurity?

*Non, mon cher. C'est Paris. Vive la différence!*

In front of the church across the street a young couple suddenly breaks stride, face each other, and fall into a passionate

embrace. Their lips meet; their mouths open. Passersby smile indulgently, appreciatively.

Borderline exhibitionism? An infantile need to prove one's sexual competency, possibly an indication of latent homosexuality?

*Non, non, mon cher. C'est le printemps, et la vie est belle.*

These are my thoughts as I sip café au lait in Les Deux Magots, waiting for the French novelist and critic Sasha Alexandrovich to join me. Twenty-six years earlier, desperately in need of help and absolutely convinced that he had come to the wrong person in the wrong place for it, Sasha had arrived red-eyed and distraught in my office in New York.

"THERE ARE no great novels written about one's wife."

These were Sasha Alexandrovich's first words to me when he sat down in my office those many years ago.

"So let's get things straight between us lest we get off to a dishonest start." He went on. "I know what you do in here, Doctor. I know all about your verbal lobotomies. You would gladly reduce us all to happy little automatons with smiles of contentment plastered to our benign kissers. Happy with the little wifey and kids. Happy with the job, with the humdrum mediocrity of our tiny, tinny, trivial lives. They call you a shrink, eh, Dr. Akeret? You would shrink my spirit and call it mental health! Shrink my passion in the name of normality! You would probably shrink my manhood, too, if you thought it would keep me home and out of trouble. If you thought it would keep me free of danger. But let me tell you something, Doctor: I live for danger! I thrive on it! It is the fire that makes my life real, that ignites my candle of creativity. Listen carefully, Doctor, I implore you: Danger is my élan vital. Tragedy is my muse. Don't even think of excising these from my life. I repeat, there are no great novels written about one's wife!"

Sasha delivered this hyperliterate tirade at a feverish pitch, gesturing manically with his long-fingered hands, his intense dark eyes boring into mine. He was a tall, slightly stooped man with shaggy hair and furrowed cheeks. He wore what were then unfashionably baggy trousers, a deep blue shirt with the top three buttons unfastened, and a silk cravat tied loosely at his neck. I had known before he arrived that Sasha was a novelist and critic of some note in the French language, but I had not anticipated such a spellbinding speaker of English. Sasha was a performer and, like most performers I had treated, probably narcissistic.

"Exactly why *did* you come here?" I asked benignly.

"Because I am dead," Sasha replied, casting his gaze to the floor.

"Dead?"

"Yes. I died ten days ago. Lost the will to live the moment that my mother died. I am numb, empty, a cipher. I feel nothing, do nothing. I cannot write a word. I am just going through the motions of living now."

I waited for Sasha to continue. That morning—a Saturday—when he phoned me, Sasha had pleaded for an emergency session as soon as possible. He had sounded out of breath, panicked. He said that he had been crying and "howling" for ten days. He had also said that he saw no more point in living. Was this high drama just to get an emergency session with me on the weekend? A manipulative first move in his relationship with his as-yet-unseen therapist? Even if it were, it was still a serious cry for help. I allotted Sasha an hour at the end of my day.

"How could Mother do this to me?" Sasha now wailed. "How could she leave me all alone in the world? Her only son! She knows how much I love her. She knows how much work I still have left to do! She could have at least waited!"

I gazed at Sasha Alexandrovich, holding back an incredulous smile. This forty-year-old international man of letters sounded very much like a spoiled five-year-old boy.

"Waited?" I echoed.

"Yes!" Sasha bellowed. "Mother could have waited until I was dead before she died herself!"

"Narcissism" no longer seemed merely a possibility.

Sasha went on to describe hearing about his mother's death in the middle of the night. He said he hated to be awakened; he slept alone in his own double-doored and shuttered bedroom. He had screamed at his wife when she entered his room and shook him awake to take the call from his sister in Paris. (This was the first I'd heard that he even had a wife.) Sasha's sister informed him that their mother had died from complications following a routine operation. At this Sasha had flung down the phone, raced to the basement in his nightshirt, dropped onto all fours, and "howled like a dog" for the rest of the night, waking his daughters.

"How many daughters do you have?" I interjected softly.

"What the hell kind of question is that?" Sasha shot back at me.

"Basically numerical," I replied, deadpan.

Sasha eyed me suspiciously. "What have we got here, a comedian? The psychoanalyst as stand-up comic?" He laughed derisively. "Well, I suppose that's appropriate, isn't it?"

"How many daughters?" I repeated. "Two, three?"

"Two!" Sasha snapped. "Why, if I may deign to inquire, do you ask?"

"Just curious," I replied, shrugging. "You told me that your mother had left you all alone."

Sasha fixed me with a venomous stare.

"My, my, do I detect a value judgment here?" He sneered sarcastically. " 'What kind of cad would say he is all alone if he has a wife and two daughters? What kind of monster would think only of himself at a time like that?' "

He paused dramatically, his right hand suspended in the air. He then abruptly turned that hand around and pointed the index finger at his temple as if it were the barrel of a pistol.

"Precisely this kind of monster, *mon cher!*" he declared. "The very kind of monster I must continue to be if I am to fulfill my promise as a chronicler of the truth and not some namby-pamby Norman Rockwell-ish scribe who pretties up the family as if it were some kind of picturesque breakfast cereal."

He leaned forward in his chair so that his fiery eyes were less than two feet away from mine; they seemed to battle mine for dominance. It was partially in response to hypnotic-eyed patients like Sasha that Freud had conceived of the idea of having his patients recline facing away from him. This technique has never been for me, though; I need to read my patients' eyes for clues at all times.

"I thought this was supposed to be a value-free zone in here," Sasha intoned sarcastically. "No devils, no angels. Just poor mortals with troubled minds and tortured hearts seeking your tender ministrations. No blame, just understanding."

Sasha was right, of course; my response to him had been critical, had been contaminated by an element of morality. But I had done this on purpose. The picture I was receiving of Sasha Alexandrovich was of a man who dominated every person, every situation he encountered. My guess was that he had been raised with the uncritical adulation of his mother and that he had cultivated that response from everyone else since. It seemed to me that the only way I could possibly get his full attention would be by resisting the traditional therapeutic role of the all-accepting parent. Further, I would have to begin resisting this role immediately, before Sasha had reflexively dismissed me as just another admiring conquest. But this tack was going to be difficult for me because like undoubtedly everyone else, I was utterly charmed by him. Sasha Alexandrovich was a dazzling talker, and any psychotherapist who denies that he cherishes the company of a talented talker is, I believe, not being honest with himself. The truth is, we therapists are in the business of listening to people talk all day long, and quite apart from any therapeutic considerations, we are connoisseurs of quality gab.

"A monster is okay with me," I said offhandedly. "As long as you really are a truth teller."

"The truth, yes. But none of your symbol-minded Freudian games. No dream interpretations. And no nonsense about my unconscious, please!"

I was not about to negotiate the terms of his therapy.

"Obviously I can't make you do anything you don't want to do," I said noncommittally.

Sasha gave me an appreciative smile. He was a consummate tester, and I had passed—at least for now.

I asked him for a brief outline of his life to date and he gladly obliged.

Sasha was born in Paris in 1928, the same year I was born in Zurich. Apparently from the moment of his birth Sasha's mother, Sonja, was obsessively devoted to her son. Because she was female, Sonja had been denied an education by her Russian-born parents; further, her marriage to Theo, Sasha's father, had been arranged and was loveless. Thus, not only did Sonja pour all her affection onto her only son, but all her ambitions and expectations as well.

"When I was about six or seven, Mother announced to me that I was going to be a writer, a great writer," Sasha told me matter-of-factly. "She said that André was my everyday name, but that my *real* name was Sasha Fydor. She said that name would have to wait until I published my first book. I had to earn it, you see, and I did."

Sonja believed that the life of the senses and the life of the imagination were mystically intertwined, so she was constantly weaving sensual scenarios for her son to participate in.

"For her, even making a bowel movement was a mystical, magical, sensual adventure," Sasha said. "She made it absolutely heavenly. She taught me the delicious art of postponement, waiting until I couldn't hold it in a moment longer and then exploding with it. I still practice that art when I have the time."

This was certainly a new one in the annals of toilet training as far as I knew. Later Sasha added that his mother would frequently insert a thermometer into his rectum to promote regularity, a practice he came to look forward to.

When he was six, Sasha was sent off to the neighborhood school, which, it turned out, was exclusively for girls.

"Mother thought that it was better academically. I can't think why the school authorities made an exception in my case, but no doubt Mamma convinced them that it would be a great privilege for them to have me there among them," Sasha said, not a trace of irony in his voice.

"Do you remember anything of that school?" I asked.

"Yes," Sasha replied, raising one eyebrow and offering me a conspiratorial smile. "It was the scene of my first *passion de coeur*. A girl by the name of Marie. Honey-colored hair, marvelous Cupid lips. And a straight, slender body lurking under that maddening pinafore."

"How old?"

Sasha burst into laughter. "No more than eight. I was a precocious lover!" he announced. "It ended badly, though. I dripped hot wax from a votive candle onto her pinafore when she refused to kiss me."

This was my first clue that Sasha was not only a precocious lover of women but a precocious torturer of them as well.

"I was a delicate child." Sasha went on a bit later. "My stomach was in a perpetual uproar, so Mamma designed a special diet for me and cooked it in an enamel pan. I still own that pan. Janet [his wife] cooks my food in it to this day. . . . During the war, when we all went into hiding, it became very difficult for Mamma to provide me with my proper diet."

This, amazingly, was how Sasha introduced the fact that his family had spent two years hiding in the windowless attic of a Paris warehouse during the German occupation—*as a footnote to his special dietary needs!* The obvious implication was that one of World War II's greatest casualties was young Sasha Alexandrovich's delicate stomach. The sheer magnitude of this man's narcissism was indeed impressive.

Four years after the liberation Sasha's father died of tuberculosis. Sasha was not quite twenty at the time; his sister, Paulette, was just fourteen. That same year Sasha came in first in his class at the École Normale Supérieure and embarked on his university career in classics and literature.

"With the literature came the beautiful women," Sasha said, his dark eyes sparkling. "The two have been ineluctably intertwined in my life ever since. Their faces are my words; my words are their faces. *Une belle phrase, une belle visage.* I adore the sound of the words that describe them. Round words, soft words. Wet words that tickle the tongue. First I devoured the women; then I re-created them on paper. Made the real fantastic, the fantastic real. My passionate heart is my inspiration, my surging penis my pen.

"Monique was the first. A Romanian medical student studying in Paris. Endocrinology, isn't that marvelous? Hormones, the internal chemistry of love and sex. I loved lying on the bed like a cadaver and letting her probe me with those silky, strong hands of hers. Palpitating here, pressing there. Absolutely delicious! She begged me to say unspeakable things while she examined me, to tell her what I was going to do to her after the examination was over: chew her stockings off her long legs, suck the juices from her succulent quim. Make the endocrinologist's hormones flow like the Volga. The vulgar Volga! The voluptuous vulva! *Ha!*

"I remember exactly the day that I met her. I was having coffee in La Coupole when she sat down on the terrace next to me. She was carrying *Gray's Anatomy*, can you believe it? Opened it right up to a cross section of the heart. My God, I was spellbound! This sloe-eyed specimen with one long bare leg stretched out in front of her and the other tucked demurely under her, this raven-haired Gypsy with magnificently rounded breasts—she was studying the human heart! I fell in love with her immediately, of course. I had to have her. I leaned across her table and said, 'If you wish to examine a beating heart, I will gladly rip mine out for you.' "

I glanced at my watch; we were already ten minutes past Sasha's allotted hour. I had no patients after him and no pressing need to return home for a while, yet if I had any strategy at all at this point, it was to set limits on Sasha's imperial ego, to let him know that I was not willing to indulge him completely as everyone else in his life apparently did. Yet how could I stop him in the middle of this story? Or more to the point, *how could I cheat myself out of the rest of this delicious story?*

Sasha saw me consult my watch. He leaned forward and fixed me with his spectacular gaze.

"Monique smiled, and without missing a beat she said, 'I have a scalpel in my purse, my dark-eyed friend.' At that I yanked open my shirt and—"

"We'll have to stop now," I interrupted softly.

For a moment Sasha stared at me incredulously; then he smiled and continued talking as if I had not said a word.

"I grabbed her hand and pressed it against my pounding—"

I abruptly stood and started for the door to my office. "Next time," I said.

Sasha's face reddened; his eyes bulged. He remained seated.

*"There are no great novels written about one's wife!"* he bellowed.

"I know, I know," I said in a weary voice, opening my office door. " 'All happy families are the same,' right?"

Sasha's face fell. In that instant all the vitality, all the intensity, all the charm vanished from it. He looked desperately unhappy and vulnerable, like a precocious child suddenly ignored by a doting mother. In fact, I believe that that is exactly how it felt to him.

"We have lots of time ahead of us," I said soothingly.

Sasha stood and marched out the door, barely looking at me.

"Perhaps," he said imperiously, as if it were a threat.

The moment Sasha left, I began to worry that I had been too tough on him for a first encounter. Patients suffering from narcissistic character disorder are notoriously difficult to treat, relentlessly testing and attempting to control the therapist, forever begging for special attention, be it praise or punishment. But above all, they are very easily wounded and given to extreme envy. By cutting Sasha off in mid-story, I was hitting this literary raconteur where it hurt the most; he would surely interpret it to mean that he had bored me. Even worse, by making a passing reference to Tolstoy (the "All happy families" line from *Anna Karenina*), I was invidiously comparing him to one of the literary greats that this Russian-French novelist surely envied. Still, I already sensed that over the long haul working with Sasha was going to be a perpetual high wire act, a balance between taking jabs at his grandiosity and fostering in him the confidence to live his life free from the uncompromising demands of his narcissistic ego. At this early point I believed that one of my primary goals was going to be to give Sasha Alexandrovich the confidence to be an ordinary mortal.

Which is precisely what Sasha was afraid of.

And the truth is, his fear that therapy would render him creatively impotent was not entirely ungrounded. There is an ever-expanding body of evidence linking mental disorders of various kinds to creative genius. In fact, it was a couple of millennia ago that Aristotle pointed out that "all of those who have been famous for their genius . . . have been inclined to insanity." The list of mentally unstable creative geniuses has grown over the years to include the great German composer Robert Schumann (who insisted that angels singing to him guided his compositions), Ludwig von Beethoven, Hector Berlioz, Vincent van Gogh, Honoré de Balzac, James Barrie, Joseph Conrad, Virginia Woolf, Edgar Allan Poe, Sylvia Plath, William Styron, and, of course, Leo Tolstoy, to name but a few. The list includes many men and women who spent long periods of their lives in solitude and despair, often in sanitoriums. It also includes many suicides.

But to say that mental illness and creative genius are "linked" is not the same as saying that the former causes the latter—or even vice versa, for that matter. The two just might be parallel results of a single cognitive "style"—the style of extreme openness, sensitivity, intensity, and imagination. To be a truly original artist, a person has to be able to make "wild" connections between ideas. He or she must be able to break through traditional aesthetic boundaries, to "color outside the lines." But such a risk-taking style also often implies certain psychological vulnerabilities, particularly to stress, loss, and rejection, all of which are well-known precipitants of mental illness. In other words, an artist's aptitude for seeing the world in unconventional ways may be equal to a weakness of defenses, what some psychologists term thin boundaries.

But what does this tell me about causality the other way around? Does it mean that helping a troubled artist-patient "shore up" his "thin boundaries" is apt to result in curtailing his ability to create in original ways? That certainly seems like a reasonable conclusion to draw. Especially when many manic-depressive artists and writers claim that they draw on the heightened sensitivity, accelerated flow of ideas, and high energy of their manic states for their best creations. And further, when many of them maintain that their most fertile "material" comes out of the Sturm und Drang of their depressions and manic episodes. I could already imagine Sasha making that claim.

I could also hear him arguing that in the grand scheme of things misery was worthwhile if it produced great art because great art was transcendent. Compared with that, a happy, satisfying life was small stuff, the small stuff that psychotherapists so avidly promote.

Still, Sasha had said that he was not creating anything at all in his current numb state. The truth is any artist who goes off the deep end is not likely to be very productive. It takes more than simply original perceptions and ideas to create original work; it takes sustained energy. I knew from experience that most of the inhabitants of mental hospitals pass their days sitting perfectly still staring at the walls. No energy, no creations of any kind. Sliding all the way into full-blown mental illness does not seem the best route to supercreativity.

Yet at this point did I have any reason to believe that Sasha Alexandrovich was sliding into full-blown mental illness? Not really. He was obviously suffering a profound depression, but for good reason: He was mourning his beloved mother, who had died only ten days earlier. That he also suffered from narcissistic character disorder seemed quite clear, but that condition does not have to degenerate into a deeper debilitating sickness. Sure, it often promotes periods of intense despair, delusions of persecution, and serial unhappy relationships, but it does not necessarily do so. More to the point, for better or for worse, people suffering from this disorder tend to be high achievers. I am quite sure that any therapist seeing Pablo Picasso would have diagnosed him as suffering from narcissistic character disorder. Picasso, too, had had a mother who filled his young head with grandiose ideas about himself; he, too, had had a series of relatively short-lived, one-sided relationships. But knowing what we do now, what psychotherapist would dare recommend Pablo Picasso for treatment? Not me.

At least I like to think not.

So what about Sasha? Right off the bat he had accused me of wanting to "shrink [his] spirit and call it mental health! Shrink [his] passion in the name of normality!" Could there be any truth in that? Is there in me (and my colleagues) an underlying conservative agenda that wants to promote ordinariness in our patients' lives because we think that "going to extremes" is bad for one's mental health? The very idea that mania is considered a pathology implies such an agenda. Why, after all, should being in this heightened state complete with inflated ideas about oneself be a sickness? Why should we, who make so much of the positive power of "self-esteem," be so critical of the swelled egos of people in the throes of mania? Because mania is almost always followed by depression? Isn't that throwing out the baby with the bath? Shouldn't we be trying to figure out how to get rid of the depression while *saving* the mania with its hyperawareness, free-flowing ideas, high energy, and super self-esteem—all excellent preconditions for creativity?

Even Freud's famous dictum that the goal of analysis is to engender an ability to "work and love" smacks of middle-class morality, a Calvinistic predilection for hard work and stable marriages. What does it say about a passionately romantic French writer who gets both his material and his drive by living at the edge? I have never written a novel in my life, but yes, I am inclined to agree that a great one is not written about one's wife.

I was going to have to feel my way on this issue. For starters, I would have to figure out what it was Sasha really wanted from therapy, which would not necessarily be the same as what he said he wanted from it. That is, if Sasha wanted to continue with therapy at all. When he had left in a huff that Saturday afternoon, we had not made any future appointments. I had my doubts that I would hear from him again.

I didn't have to wait long. The following morning he called me on my home phone.

"I want to make two appointments for next week," Sasha said in a formal, rather imperious voice. "Let me advise you as to my availability."

We worked out the dates, and I hung up smiling. God help me, I was already looking forward to some good stories.

"I refuse to speak about my mother," Sasha informed me before he was even seated. "I know how terribly disappointed you must be, Doctor. You probably have your Oedipus complex trap all set and baited, ready to grab me by the balls. So that you can dissect me according to plan, according to your pat formula. Yes, I am awfully sorry to disappoint you, but you see, Doctor, if there was ever a man who did *not* have an Oedipus complex, it is I!"

I nodded my very best, professional, noncommittal nod.

*"Don't you believe me?"* Sasha said, raising his voice aggressively.

"I don't know," I replied, shrugging. "I'm not always sure that it's that useful a concept. It covers a lot of ground. Sometimes it appears that *everyone* has an Oedipus complex."

"Not everyone!" Sasha retorted defiantly.

This time I made no attempt to suppress my grin. "There was a joke that was going around the White Institute a few years back," I said, smiling at Sasha. "It was about this forty-year-old man who still lived with his mother. Well, one day he went to a psychoanalyst, and when he came home, he told his mother that the analyst said he suffered from an Oedipus complex. 'Oedipus, Shmedipus!' his mother cried. 'As long as you love your mother!' "

Sasha did not so much as smile.

"Let's not waste any more time," he said. "I find myself in a rather interesting dilemma, and I need your help sorting things out."

"Tell me about it."

"I am in love. Deeply, passionately, *flagrantly* in love. I am delirious with it. I am sick with it. I have never felt more alive in my life. Her name is Eva. She is from Stockholm, all fire and ice. A goddess. I met her in Paris last August at the Comparative Literature Congress. She is a Strindberg expert. *My God, Strindberg!* Fate is so cunning. Any other Scandinavian writer—Lagerkvist, Ibsen—I could have had my little dalliance and moved on in sweet oblivion. But Eva quotes whole passages from the *The Dream Play* while we are in bed. Recites them in Swedish while I run my hands over her magnificent rump, while I ski those Swedish Alps. How could I possibly get her out of my mind?"

I found myself listening with bemusement. Only five days earlier Sasha had declared that he was numb, motiveless, dead. Today he was convinced that he had never felt more alive in his life. Apparently the period of mourning his mother was over.

"There are complications, of course, not the least of which is geography. She wants me to come to Stockholm. She runs a literary agency there. She says I can write full-time; she earns more than enough to support us both. But there is no light in winter there. Murky days, endless inky nights. I shall go mad yearning for the sun. 'The Sun, the Sun. Give me the Sun!' And then, of course, there is her husband, Gunnar. Can anyone possibly be married to a man named Gunnar? Blond and blue-eyed. *'More blond than I.'* Ha! The little Russian half Jew makes her scream for more while Gunnar the Gargantuan leaves her cold. Gunnar the Viking with horns in his helmet. And I put them there!"

Here Sasha burst into a triumphant cackle before continuing.

"And then there is Janet, the mother of my children. She is a saint, of course. A martyr of biblical proportions. They should build a statue of her in Lorraine next to Jeanne d'Arc. No, no, they needn't *build* a statue, she already *is* a statue! Cast in stone! Cold, impenetrable stone! But she cannot be ignored. No, she must be dealt with somehow."

"Does your wife know about Eva?" I asked.

Sasha shrugged in true Gallic fashion, pursing his lips, arching his eyebrows.

"She does know about my little indiscretions with my students. My private tutorials in literature, teaching those rosy-cheeked American college girls how to distinguish between sensation and sentiment. She knows about these, yet she turns a blind eye. But with Eva it is an altogether different story. It is a grand passion, not a mere distraction. I have taken great care to hide all traces of her from Janet. Eva's letters and calls come to my office at the university. And Sunday, when she flew in for a visit, I told Janet that I had a meeting in Boston."

"You mean to say that Eva flew in from Stockholm this weekend?" I asked.

"But of course," Sasha said, grinning proudly. "I told her how much I was suffering with Mamma's death, so she booked the first flight to New York. We spent twenty-four hours locked in a bedroom at the Earle Hotel in the Village. A room straight out of Genet—paint peeling, radiators clanging. We went at it to exhaustion; then we sent out for Peking duck, scarfed it down, and went at it again. Duck and fuck, fuck and duck! *Ha!* My glorious ice goddess forsook her palatial digs in Gamla Stan to suck my cock in the Earle Hotel. I tell you, Doctor, she is far better therapy than you are."

I gazed back at him impassively. Sasha seemed uncomfortable with my lack of response.

"Have I told you about her glorious derriere?" he said urgently.

"Yes," I replied coolly. "Like skiing the Swedish Alps, if I'm not mistaken."

"Have *you* ever had such a woman, Doctor?" Sasha asked, tilting his head back arrogantly.

"I don't think that's relevant," I replied.

*"Not relevant?"* Sasha bellowed. "A woman like that—with flaxen hair hanging down to the crack in her ass? If you can say that such a woman is not relevant, it is quite obvious that you have never experienced anything remotely like her. Why don't you just admit it?"

I said nothing, showed nothing. Sasha was once again baiting me. His sexual competitiveness was as unsubtle as an adolescent's. And like an adolescent's, Sasha's recounting of his sexual exploits seemed at least as important to him as the sexual experience itself. Such sexual braggadocio in a man of forty suggested some fairly deep-seated sexual insecurity, which was consistent with my diagnosis of narcissistic character disorder. Lurking just below the surface in narcissistic womanizers—the Don Juans of the world—one usually finds a person who fears that he is sexually inadequate.

What is more, the pattern that was emerging from Sasha's womanizing stories strongly suggested a classic Madonna-whore complex—the splitting of the female world into saintly untouchable mothers and tawdry bedable tarts. Sufferers from this complex usually marry the former and have sex with them as little as possible but do "unspeakable" things with the latter. According to this theory, the Madonnas are stand-ins for these men's own untouchable mothers. This, of course, implied something seriously Oedipal in Sasha's psychology, not a notion that he was eager to discuss with me.

"Exactly how can I help you, Sasha?" I asked quietly.

Sasha seemed almost startled by the question. He furrowed his brow a moment, started to speak, stopped, and started again.

"I, uh, I sometimes feel guilty about how monstrous I am being to Janet and the children," he stammered, clearly embarrassed by the idea that he should feel guilt about anything at all. "And I need your help dealing with that. You know—getting rid of it."

"Do you want me to grant you absolution?" I asked, deadpan. "Like the pope?"

"Look, it's obviously neurotic; all guilt is," Sasha said impatiently. "So do whatever it is you do to ferret it out."

"But without mentioning your mother, right?" I said evenly.

Sasha narrowed his eyes contemptuously. "Look, Doctor, if you don't feel up to the task, let me know now, so we don't end up wasting any more of each other's time."

I took a deep breath. The last thing I want to do with any patient is to try to sell him on my efficacy as a therapist, but especially not with someone like Sasha, who might fail to improve just to spite me.

"I'm sorry," I said. "But how things go in here doesn't really have that much to do with me."

"I thought as much!" Sasha snorted.

I checked my watch. Time was up.

"So, how's your writing going?" I asked casually as I started to rise from my chair.

Once again I witnessed the vitality drain from Sasha's face and be replaced by an expression of utter hopelessness. He stood and left my office without another word.

I found myself feeling relieved by Sasha's response to that question. He was still blocked creatively, and clearly he could not blame it on our two rather superficial sessions of psychotherapy; I could put my internal debate on "art versus sanity" on hold, at least for the time being.

But the question of how to work with Sasha still eluded me. All patients put up resistance to therapy; getting beyond it is fundamental to the work we do. But Sasha's resistance was in a category by itself. The ground rules he had laid down— no talking about his mother, no techniques that smacked of the standard psychoanalytic repertoire, such as dream analysis or free association—made therapy as I practiced it virtually impossible. But Sasha insisted that he did not want ordinary therapy. No, he wanted surgery: Snip out the guilt; make over the monster.

Did he really believe that this was possible? Did he think that we could do a little psychic "snipping" and "tinkering" and have him running smoothly without his having to dig very deeply at all? It was hard to know. Sasha was a highly intelligent, sophisticated man, yet at the same time he was convinced that he could not possibly have an Oedipus complex.

What did he think he was really coming to me for? Simply to help him "sort out" his complicated social life? He didn't need me for that, and he knew it. Did he come to my office just to impress me with his fabulous exploits? I certainly doubted that, too; he had whole classrooms of eager college girls for that.

What did he want from me?

I had only one clue, and I had detected it in his deep-set eyes both times that I saw his face suddenly go lifeless. Then I glimpsed in him such a profound sense of loss that I was sure it went far beyond his guilt over his extramarital affairs or even his grief over his mother's death. At those moments his face had the haunted, terrified look of a figure in an Edvard Munch painting. For those few moments I did not see a self-aggrandizing, woman-obsessed, vile monster. No, what I saw was a man fighting for his life.

All I could do for now is let Sasha Alexandrovich tell me his stories. Their plots were rapidly thickening.

"WHAT I ADORE about Eva are her contradictions," Sasha said excitedly a few sessions later. "She has those terrifying blond bangs that look like a Prussian helmet. So militant, so severe. But when she opens her mouth, out come these little breathy whispers like wisps of fog. So reticent, so demure. She towers over me like a Valkyrie, and then she curls up at my feet like a kitten. But best is the contradiction between Eva with her clothes on and Eva with her clothes off. She is like Catherine Deneuve in *Belle de Jour*, a woman of elegance in her tailored suits and pearl necklaces. But close the door and unwrap her, and she is a beast, a tigress. No shame. She crouches on the floor and waves that awesome bum in the air for me to drill into. She knows how much I love that. The back door, the forbidden cave."

It was little wonder that Sasha had a predilection for anal sex, given what I knew about his mother's devotion to fun and games in the bowel department. It also sounded as if Sasha were attracted to the forbiddenness of it: breaking the taboo, being a naughty boy. I imagined that there was an element of sadism that appealed to him, too; anal sex can be quite painful for the "receiving" partner. But perhaps most significant, anal sex makes any kind of personal intimacy virtually impossible: no eye contact, no kissing, no hugging. It is all genital: thrilling but ultimately lonely-making. This is the price narcissists pay in every aspect of their relationships.

As usual I kept these observations to myself lest Sasha think I was being too "psychoanalytic."

"And, Janet, does she enjoy anal sex, too?" I asked.

"She despises it!" Sasha barked. "She says it's unclean, unnatural. Unnatural? What does that American prig know about nature? About the beast that lurks in all of us? She thinks making love is like setting a table: The fork goes here, the knife goes there. I have to pester her if I want to do it my way, and then all the joy is taken out of it. I never have to pester Eva."

"Do you make love to Janet at all?" I asked.

"Hardly ever," Sasha replied. "Sometimes I'll go through the motions just to expiate my guilt."

I asked Sasha if his relationship with Janet had ever been passionate, and he said that at the beginning it had been but that she had changed after they were married. I asked him to describe those earlier days with Janet, and he told me about meeting her when she was on a Fulbright at the Sorbonne.

"What fabulous legs that girl had!" Sasha said, suddenly warming to his subject. "Long and lean like a racehorse. Muscular in that quintessential American way. She had been a gymnast as a child. So earnest she was. So eager to learn. And of course, I was eager to teach her.

"I begged her to stay on with me after her fellowship expired, but she had a position waiting for her at Columbia University and didn't want to risk losing it. As if that could possibly mean more than an affair of the heart. My God, I should have known then that her American practicality would obliterate any vestige of real feeling. There were desperate transatlantic phone calls, of course. Long letters, telegrams. Surprise flights in the middle of the night. I implored her to stay with me. To stop denying destiny. In the end nothing would budge her but a proposal of marriage. I might just as well have proposed a double suicide."

"You seem to have a taste for transatlantic romances," I said, but even this little observation seemed to tread too close to "psychological interpretation."

"Such romances are inevitable. I am an international man," Sasha responded firmly.

"Don't you think there might be something about the distance itself—the remoteness, the unavailability—that makes these women more desirable?" I said.

"Good Lord, Akeret, is this your idea of a profound psychological insight?" Sasha intoned sarcastically. "That absence makes the heart grow fonder? I knew Freud was banal, but this is less than banal: It is trivial!"

"I'm saying a bit more than that," I ventured. "That maybe there is a pattern here. Like that your long-distance romances tend to lose their luster once you're finally living together. You see, where there are patterns of behavior—repetitions—there is usually something in your past that—"

"Christ, Akeret, do you make this stuff up as you go along?"

"Some of it, yes," I replied, smiling.

Sasha laughed, surprised by my candor. But that is as far as he was willing to take my psychological "insights" for the day.

At this point he launched into a new, highly dramatic story, this one about Janet's discovering a love note from Eva in his coat pocket and his convincing Janet that it was from a literary "fan" he had never met. I listened with growing apprehension. For me, this story was handwriting on the wall: I was sure that Sasha was unconsciously setting things up so that his affair would be found out. He was turning up the heat on his personal potboiler, and I was certain there would be heavy damage done to everyone—Sasha included—before it was over.

If Sasha had been any other of my patients, I would have pointed this out to him. I would have suggested that rather than determine his future for himself, he was creating a drama in which he could be only observer and victim. I would have told him that this was one more example of how he was not free at all, that he was a prisoner of his neurosis.

But I did not say a word. Because it was at that point that I realized how I was going to work with Sasha: I was going to let him self-destruct. I was going to sit back and watch as he courted his "élan vital," danger, and tempted his "muse," tragedy—his two necessities for the grand creative life. Maybe then the pain of living would become so intense that we could start psychotherapy.

It was not as if I had much choice anyhow.

I FELT AS IF I were watching a train wreck in slow motion.

The following week Sasha came stumbling into my office looking wild-eyed and disheveled. Without having discussed it with Sasha, Eva had separated from her husband.

"She said that after she was with me, Gunnar's touch made her flesh crawl," Sasha told me. "She says that I have made it impossible for her ever to be with another man again. She has been permanently imprinted by me. *Branded* was the word she used. What a word, eh? *Branded!*"

Sasha delivered this news with obvious pride, but the flutter of trepidation lurking just beneath that pride was all too obvious to me. I nodded noncommittally as he excitedly ram-

bled on. Toward the end of the session Sasha said he had begun
feeling his literary imagination "yawning and stretching"
lately.

"The sleeping giant may be waking at last," he said.

A few sessions later Sasha reported that something had been
coming over Janet lately, and it worried him.

"She walks around as if she is drugged," he told me. "Her
face is drawn; her eyes are half closed. She looks like a zombie.
She's stopped cooking for me altogether. And she just pours
things out of the can for the girls. Sometimes she never gets
out of her nightdress all day long. Do you think she's sick?"

"Maybe," I said. "Or maybe she's depressed."

Sasha considered this a moment; the idea obviously had
not occurred to him.

"Why would she be depressed?" he asked ingenuously.

"I don't know," I said. "I don't know her."

"Sometimes I wish she would have an affair herself," he
said. "Then maybe I wouldn't feel so guilty myself."

That look of utter despair flashed across Sasha's face again,
but in a moment it was gone, and he was talking about his
latest transatlantic erotic conversation with his Swedish
lover.

Not many days after that Sasha came to my office looking
terribly distraught and tired. It seems that Eva had flown into
New York unannounced and they had made delirious love for
an entire weekend in his favorite tawdry hotel room, but on
Sunday night, just as she was about to leave, Eva had suddenly
become surly.

"Out of the blue she demanded to know if I had spoken to
Janet about a divorce yet," Sasha told me. "Outrageous! I
never said anything about divorcing Janet. Why do women
always have to turn pleasure into travail? The sublime into the
banal? They can't have sex without thinking about babies!"

I stuck to my MO and said nothing, pointed out no patterns,
issued no warnings. I felt like the Narrator in Anouilh's *Anti-*

*gone:* I knew that the spring of fate was tightly wound, and all I could do was stand by as the tragedy unfolded.

Sasha arrived at his next session looking more distressed than ever. Without warning, Janet herself had gone into psychotherapy five days a week.

"With a woman therapist!" Sasha raged.

"It's been known to happen," I said.

"But I don't believe this one's a therapist at all. She's a sorceress. *A Svengali!*"

It was an interesting pejorative allusion for a man who went through life attempting to mesmerize and enslave women. But of course, I said nothing.

"Janet is not herself anymore. She goes out willy-nilly, leaving the children to fend for themselves. She never cooks, never cleans. And the things that come out of her mouth—the crudeness. The—the disrespect!"

"Is she disrespectful of you?" I asked.

"Yes, of me. Of my work. Even, God forgive her, of my departed mother. Is this what your famous psychotherapy does? Turn civilized women into monsters?"

I had to summon every ounce of professional restraint not to smile at this one: Sasha Alexandrovich, the man who was terrified that psychotherapy would tame the monster in him, was now accusing therapy of *promoting* monsterhood. But this was only a problem in someone else, of course. In the solipsistic universe of an inveterate narcissist, what's good for oneself is rarely good for anyone the narcissist has to deal with, especially not for someone he has to live with.

I was intrigued by what was happening to Sasha's wife. Obviously she *had* been depressed, probably precipitated by all the neglect, repression, and disloyalty of her husband. It seemed that therapy had already begun to give her back some self-respect, and with it the ego strength to assert herself. This was a twist of the plot I had not anticipated. I had an inkling it might pay off in my work with Sasha. Perhaps his compulsive one-upmanship with women would extend to psychotherapy itself: Sasha could devote himself to becoming a "superior" patient to Janet.

But first the pot had to boil more furiously. Events began picking up speed.

The following week Sasha attended a three-day conference in Paris. Eva met him there, but things did not go well. She insisted that he make love to her without contraception; she wanted his baby. When Sasha refused, she would not let him touch her. Then she began to insult him, several times in front of his colleagues. She accused him of being old and worn out, a has-been writer. She flirted brazenly with some of the younger writers at the conference. But on their last night together Eva broke down and begged his forgiveness. They had made love until dawn when he had to catch his plane.

In the meantime, life with Janet continued to baffle him.

"She wasn't even home when I got back from Paris," he complained. "Out with her new friends, while I'm supposed to baby-sit!"

Janet had taken her first job in years, as an editor of a left-wing weekly, and was now frequently out in the evenings. When she came home late that night, Sasha had suggested they make love, but she had said that she wasn't in the mood and had closed her bedroom door in his face.

"She didn't even want to talk with me," Sasha said. "At least we used to have that in common—intellectual companionship. But now nothing. I wonder if she is having an affair. My God, how could she not want me?"

True to form, Sasha wanted what he couldn't have. Now forbidden, his wife was suddenly desirable.

At the end of this session Sasha told me that he had begun taking notes for a new novel.

During the following three weeks Sasha was in perpetual turmoil, endlessly debating his alternatives: "If I marry Eva, I'll have two families to support. I won't be able to afford anything for myself, none of my special indulgences. And anyway, how can I leave my daughters, my own flesh and blood? But still, Eva is everything I desire: wild sex, youth, glorious youth! Janet is beginning to show that wear and tear that is so unappealing in older women. If I stay with her, I will wither myself. The ink in my pen will dry up. I could never be faithful to Janet. But then, could I be to Eva? Why marry again if I am just going to be unfaithful again?"

A good question. Sasha was getting his first faint glimmerings of what it meant to be caught in a repeating pattern. I still said nothing.

Then, virtually simultaneously, the stories of Eva and Janet reached dramatic climaxes.

Eva had flown in for another weekend visit at the Hotel Earle. They had made love, then Sasha had gone out to get food, and when he returned, he found Eva standing naked on the ledge of an open window, threatening to jump if he did not marry her.

"I had no choice. I promised her I would marry her, although I knew as I said it that it was a lie. I could never marry Eva. She is too crazy, too demanding. But I said, 'Yes, yes, of course, anything, my darling, just come inside.' She finally came back in, and we made love again. Then I toddled her off to her plane. But just as I was leaving her, she looked at me with those baby blue eyes and said, 'Sasha, if you don't keep your promise, I will kill you.' So sweetly, she said it, so sweetly that I knew she meant it."

When Sasha returned home that evening, he confessed to Janet about his affair.

"And [Janet] burst out laughing," Sasha told me. "Can you believe it? She said, 'Let me guess, with a little blond child who cries every time you leave her? I hope you are enjoying it, Sasha. I hope you are enjoying it half as much as I am enjoying my affair!' "

Janet then told Sasha that she was sleeping with a colleague at work, a black writer by the name of Hugo.

"*Un nègre!*" Sasha wailed. "Probably endowed like a stallion. And putting it to *my* Janet! She is mine, damn it! Mine! Mine!"

Sasha ranted on for most of the hour. He could not quite believe what had happened.

"They are monsters, both of them monsters!" he cried. "Crueler than I have ever been to either of them. Torturers! Sadists! *Women!*"

For the first time in his life Sasha had been "outmonstered."

When our time was almost up, Sasha abruptly became silent. He looked over at me like a defeated child.

"I had a nightmare last night," he said softly.

I nodded for him to go on, and Sasha described the following dream: A man is using napalm to maim and kill women and children. (This was 1971, the height of the Vietnam War.) Sasha is enlisted by authorities to capture this man and turn him in. Sasha finds him, but suddenly the man metamorphoses into a beautiful woman, and Sasha begins to make love to her. She pleads with him not to turn her in, and Sasha promises not to. Suddenly the beautiful woman transforms back into the killer and escapes.

After Sasha was finished recounting the dream, I looked at him inquiringly. This was a critical moment in our work; I needed to proceed with caution.

"So, what does it mean, Doctor?" Sasha said, his voice suddenly soaked with sarcasm. "That I'm in love with my mother and want to murder my father?"

"You've got me." I shrugged.

"Good God, do you mean to say that I finally tell you a dream and you don't have a clue what it means?" Sasha said tauntingly. "What exactly did they teach you in graduate school?"

"That what means one thing to one person probably means something quite different to another," I replied mildly.

"Or that it means nothing at all," Sasha retorted.

"Maybe," I said. "In psychotherapy we're stuck with the same ambiguity that you're stuck with in literature. No fixed facts to lead the way. Just hunches."

This was not a thought that I had articulated for myself in quite this way before, but it felt right on the mark as I said it. Sasha gazed back at me with a stunned expression. I think what I had said went straight to the heart of his skepticism about therapy. Or perhaps the personal disasters tumbling all around him had finally made him vulnerable to hearing something that I had been trying to tell him all along; that was, after all, my purpose in not interfering in his "train wreck."

With very little prodding or coaching, Sasha abruptly began to interpret his dream on his own, skipping from one association to another as he constructed a many-leveled analysis that placed his current personal calamities in the context of critical events of his childhood. As I always suspected, Sasha had an exceptional gift for dream analysis. It is, after all, in the same ball park as literary analysis.

Sasha related the dream back to his mother: "She would never 'turn me in' for anything, no matter how horrendous I'd behaved. Never tell on me to my father. I used to push it, to see just how impossible I could be without being punished. But I knew, like the woman in the dream, that I could always seduce Mamma, that I could always get away with murder."

He also related the dream back to his experience of being saved during the Second World War: "I recently saw a photograph of a Vietnamese child who'd been burned by napalm. I not only felt terrible pity for that poor child, I felt this incredible guilt, too. It's survivor's guilt, I'm sure. So many children died in the Holocaust, but not me."

A little later: "Sometimes it feels like I am napalming

my own children. By never being there. Always abandoning them."

And later, "I see 'Cupid and Psyche' in the dream—you know, the original 'Beauty and the Beast.' The metamorphosis, the transformation. I am the Beast, of course. Condemned to ugliness for my sins, waiting for an innocent virgin to make me beautiful again. Chesterton said that the Beast must be loved *before* it is lovable. That's me, all right. But what about now that Mamma is dead? Who can make me lovable now?"

I said nothing.

"Aha! So you think I am unlovable, too!" Sasha exclaimed.

"Not at all," I replied. "I was just thinking how you let that napalm killer in your dream escape only to continue wreaking havoc. You know, of course, that your lovability is your choice and yours alone. Only you can decide if you want to let the Beast in you have his way."

Sasha was thoughtful a moment, then went on interpreting his dream from a dozen more different points of view. We were well past his hour, and there was another patient waiting, but this one time I let Sasha go on as long as he wanted. When he finally finished, there was a look of almost childlike wonder on his face. After six months psychotherapy had begun.

"I HAVE BEEN WRITING nonstop for three days," Sasha said excitedly as he sat down for our next session. "It flows out of me like fresh blood. Oh, what a glorious feeling it is. My heart is beating again. I feel young, alive. I am my brilliant self again."

He went on to tell me that he had awakened the day after our last session with the "organizing image" of his new novel in his mind's eye: A man opens his front door and finds the severed head of his first wife on his doorstep. The novel was to be a psychological mystery about a man who very gradually discovers that he himself is a murderer.

"He discovers this by plunging deeper and deeper into his unconscious," Sasha told me.

I was, of course, tremendously gratified by this turn of events. Not only was Sasha a "convert" to the psychotherapeutic process, but he was already using it to overcome his writer's block. Therapy had not killed his creative drive; it was facilitating it. What is more, it seemed one could, after all, write a great novel about one's wife, albeit a decapitated one.

Sasha removed a notebook from his pocket and flipped it open. He had recorded several dreams that he wanted to discuss, and that is what we did for the rest of that hour, exploring areas of his life that he had never mentioned before: his fear and jealousy of his father, his sense of physical inferiority, his childhood preoccupation with death and dead animals. As before, Sasha's analysis of his dreams was wide-ranging and brilliant, full of clues to his adult obsessions and patterns of relationships.

As he was about to leave at the end of this hour, Sasha said, "By the way, I've moved out of the house. Janet is filing for divorce."

This, that day, was incidental news.

AND SO IT WENT for the next two years. Sasha became my star patient, digging, analyzing, associating, discovering himself in all his complexity. He began to understand why he was forever locking himself in "enslavement relationships." He started to feel "in his blood" how his narcissism could never be completely satisfied, especially now that his mother was dead. Further, he started to see how his narcissism could doom him to perpetual loneliness, no matter how many passionate affairs he had.

During these two years he was divorced from Janet, his relationship with Eva ended (in a public brawl in a Paris brasserie), and he began a new relationship with a young American graduate student. Also during this period he finished writing his new novel, *La Bête (The Beast)*. It was a book that I had literally watched being written; he often pulled out a notebook and took long notes for it during our sessions. Along the way Sasha told me that I was a principal character in the book; he had made me the protagonist's therapist.

*La Bête* was hailed as a work of genius by Sasha's publisher in Paris. Prepublication readings by colleagues and critics confirmed this evaluation. Not long after Sasha received this news, he went to Paris to meet with his publisher. Sasha called me from the airport as soon as he got back. He needed an emergency session, he said. I agreed to see him that evening.

When Sasha walked into my office, I realized that I had not seen that expression of utter desolation on his face for more than a year now. But here it was again, more devastating-looking than ever. For the first time ever Sasha was silent when he sat down. I waited, then asked how things had gone in Paris.

"Fine," he said dismissively. "Everybody adores the book. They've already sold the foreign rights in four languages."

Then he went silent again for several minutes. Finally he said, "I had a terrifying dream my next to last night in Paris. It was the anniversary of my mother's death. I woke up soaking wet, shivering."

This was the dream: "I am in the office of a French psychoanalyst, and he tells me that I am wasting my time seeing an American therapist. Too superficial, the analyst says. No soul. The analyst holds up a page—it's from my manuscript—and he says, 'You have to go behind the letters or you will never discover their true meaning.'

"Then I realize that we are in a graveyard. My mother is next to me, and we are both in black, in mourning. My mother says, 'You have accomplished so much.' And I turn to my mother and say, 'I am nothing. I do not exist.' "

That is when he woke up shivering.

"I could feel it then, feel that I do not exist at all. Because what's the point, really? Write some books, make love to some women. None of it really means anything in the end. You can write a hundred books, and when you're dead, what difference does any of it make? What does it add up to?"

My first thought was that Sasha was suffering a "postpartum" depression after delivering his book and that I should have anticipated this, helped him to prepare for it. I knew many writers experienced such a devastating letdown after finishing a long work. Virginia Woolf was said to be so deeply depressed when she finished writing a book that she could not get out of bed for months.

But I sensed there was something more than that going on with Sasha and that it was, indeed, something that we had not touched in our two-plus years of therapy. His dream was very clear on that score: We had missed a crucial element in our work, something fundamental to Sasha's being in the world.

"What do you suppose *is* behind the letters?" I asked him.

Sasha offered me a sad smile.

"It's a lovely dream, isn't it?" he said bitterly. "So literary. It is asking me to look at the subtext of my own work, the meaning behind my own words. So I did. I spent the last two days looking very deeply, very astutely. And do you know what I find behind that screen of marvelous words? Absolutely nothing! A person who never existed. A would-be life. *My own!*"

Sasha began to weep, something I had never witnessed in his over two years of therapy. At first he cried softly, but soon it built to racking sobs that shook him violently. This went on for several minutes. Watching Sasha's handsome face contort in pain, I suddenly knew exactly what it was that we had missed in our work together, and I realized that he knew what that was, too.

In a fundamental existential sense, Sasha had sacrificed his life to his art. His book about his life was more real to him than the life that had inspired it. In the end the ecstasy and torture of his love affairs were nothing more than letters on a page. He experienced everything in his life as a story; even the depth therapy we had worked through was part of that story, "material" for it. So in the end there was no substance, no real life behind the words. In the end the author of his autobiographical novel did not exist.

This was the flip side of the "art versus sanity" problem, a side that neither Sasha nor I had ever acknowledged. Yes, perhaps "mental health" can curtail the creative process, but perhaps the creative process can curtail a fully lived life.

It can be argued that all of us distance ourselves from our lives to some degree by turning our experiences into anecdotes and stories, if only the stories that we tell ourselves and stash in our "libraries" of memory. There is some truth in this, of course. But I believe that what had been revealed to Sasha in this dream was a genuine crisis of being: Somewhere deep in his unconscious he felt that he was missing from his own life. A major part of the reason that I believed this crisis was real for him was that look of profound loss that I had seen on Sasha's face when he first started therapy and that I saw again this day. That expression had vanished when he started to write again, when his life *became* a novel, but now that the book was finished, that look of devastating loss was back. Therapy had helped him to write again, but now that the book was done, Sasha ceased to have a life that felt completely real to him.

We spent many hours in the following months talking about this dream and the existential crisis it represented for Sasha. It is the subtlest of problems, one of pure phenomenology, yet it goes to the core of one's life. Sasha and I discussed the psychological reasons why he might be driven to retreat from being in the world in an unmediated way, from being, as he put it, "engaged in his own life." The reasons we found were compelling, fascinating, but always, after discussing them, Sasha would came back to the same thought: No life, not even his own, could ever be more sublime than a great work of art.

We were still wrestling with this issue when Sasha received

a prestigious appointment at the University of Paris. He had been in therapy with me for over three years at that point. He was involved now with yet another young woman, and he had begun work on a new novel. It was about a man who discovers that he does not exist.

At the end of our last session Sasha embraced me and kissed me on both cheeks.

"On behalf of the books, I thank you," he said.

I DID NOT RECOGNIZE Sasha at first when I saw him shuffling toward me on the Boulevard St.-Germain. What I saw was a stooped, gray-haired man with a plastic hearing aid protruding from his right ear, a man, as the French say, in the *troisième âge*. Sasha is, of course, exactly as old as I am. A sobering thought, that. I stood.

"Hello, Sasha."

He kissed me on both cheeks, then sat down at my café table with obvious difficulty.

"It is so good to see you, Robert," he said, smiling. "I think of you often. Like a great love affair."

I grinned. He was ever the seducer; that, obviously, had not changed. I noticed that patrons all around the terrace had looked up when Sasha arrived. Some nodded and smiled. Sasha nodded back rather stiffly.

"I have a new book out," Sasha said, leaning toward me confidentially. "I'm on TV, in the papers. So everybody knows me. In France we still treat our writers like celebrities."

"Congratulations," I said.

Sasha shrugged.

"Yes, the writer has flourished," he said ruefully. "You did something extraordinarily important for me, Robert. You liberated the repressed writer in me. You helped me accomplish my mother's wish."

"And the man, how is he doing?"

"Good old Robert. Always gets right to the nub of things."

Sasha laughed, then gazed down at the table a moment. "No, the man has not fared so well as the writer. Especially not the body of the man."

"You're ill?"

"Yes and no," Sasha replied. "One doctor I saw said, 'You have no fatal illness in you, Alexandrovich, yet total dysfunction is setting in.' I am half alive. To digest, I have to take pills. To sleep, I take more pills. To defecate, I have to take medicine at night. Even to make love, I have to give myself an injection. As I say in my new novel, I am a technological doll."

"I'm sorry to hear that."

"My doctor says it's all psychosomatic." Sasha went on in a bemused tone. "I asked him what that meant, and he said, 'It means you can either take antidepressants or go back into analysis.' So there's another pill for me, a French antidepressant. The worst part of it is that it means I can't drink wine anymore."

Sasha smiled at me.

"Do you remember that I used to say there are no great novels written about one's wife?" he asked.

"Of course, I do."

"Well, in my last book I wrote all about an old man's infirmities. Now that's the stuff of great literature, eh?"

The waiter came by. I ordered another café au lait, and Sasha asked for a mineral water with lemon. The waiter then leaned over and whispered something into Sasha's ear.

"A devotee," Sasha said, smiling, after the waiter had left. "He read about me in yesterday's *Le Monde*. He says that only I am willing to say what men really think."

"And what's that?"

"Basically that no woman over forty is worth making love to," Sasha said matter-of-factly. "I don't see what is so scandalous about that. One of my colleagues, a professor who is married to a student half his age, sets the limit at thirty-five, so actually I think I am quite enlightened.

"I simply write the truth as I see it, Robert. To me, a woman should be about thirty or forty. She has to have a smooth face and breasts that are just so. Listen, I cannot change myself. Perhaps I am master of my actions, but I absolutely am not the master of my des es. Whoever says he is is a liar. And desires are not a subject ne should lie about. Certainly you must agree with that. If I learned nothing else from you, it is to dig down for the truth, no matter how monstrous it is.

"There was one reviewer, a woman *d'un certain âge*, who came to interview me, and she said, 'May I be frank with you, Alexandrovich?' And I said, 'But of course. If I write the books that I do, I certainly must allow you to be frank, too.' Well, I expected her to say the usual, what a vile male chauvinist pig I am. I have endured worse abuse, much worse. But she said, 'I was hurt by what you said about women over forty. I am over forty myself. So I asked my husband, "If something happened to me and you wanted to remarry, would you marry a woman my age or younger?" And he said, "A younger one, of course!" ' The truth will either set you free or kill you. Or maybe it will do both at the same time."

Sasha laughed softly.

"I know what you are thinking, Robert." He went on. "What a peculiar attitude for a man who needs an injection to get it up. Well, yes, it is a peculiar attitude, but it is mine, you see, so I write about it."

Sasha removed a newspaper clipping from his jacket pocket, changed from one pair of glasses to another, and began to read, translating as he went along: "[Alexandrovich's] new novel is about a vampire who sucks the blood of young people. Every book is thus the agent of a transfiguration where the writer transforms the aged professor into a young man, again ready for another existence. I feel [Alexandrovich] the writer is a vampire on top of [Alexandrovich] the man who tears him to pieces, cuts through him, eviscerates him, in order to nourish his inspiration."

Sasha set the clipping down on the table.

"This isn't news to you," he said. "We came to the same pathetic conclusion over twenty years ago, didn't we?"

I nodded.

"I haven't really changed, Robert," he announced solemnly. "I hope that doesn't disappoint you too much. Hope it doesn't ruin *your* book. Ultimately I am the same man I was then—torn, divided. Still getting by. But now the man is totally lonely. My sister lives in England. My daughters are in New York. Since my last wife, Maria, died, I have no one. Maria was an exceptional cook; she'd make these fabulous dinners, and we'd have people over. Now I don't belong to any circle, no writers, no one. I send my new books to old friends, but no one responds. I eat later and later, some nights at eleven o'clock, which is unhealthy. I go to bed at twelve-thirty after watching late shows. So you see, I am well known but lonely. And as they say, a lonely man is in very bad company. The loneliness is appalling, but I suppose that it must correspond to my desires, eh? I mean, consider the alternative: accommodating someone!"

There was more than a trace of self-pity in Sasha's voice as he spoke about his loneliness. *That* was new.

"Tell me about your books," I said after a moment.

Sasha's expression brightened immediately.

"Well, you are a running character in them," he said. "If I were to ask just about anybody in this café who Robert Akeret is, they would say, 'Why, he is Chekonieff's therapist.' Chekonieff is the name I give myself in my novels—my stand-in. But in a sense you are my stand-in, too. You have become part of me; I possess you in my imagination. Or perhaps it is I who am possessed by you. That is the question, uh? When two consciousnesses commingle, who's in charge?"

Sasha laughed.

"It is a shame you do not read French." He went on. "Or perhaps it is a blessing. You would probably be appalled by some of the thoughts that I put in your mouth. In *La Bête*, there are two hundred and fifty pages devoted to our analysis of a dream I actually had. It was not a dream that we ever worked on together, so I had to guess at what you would say. So that means that therapy was successful after all, doesn't it? If I am able to continue to do my own analysis without you? Put that in your book, Robert: Therapy was totally successful with Sasha Alexandrovich! Ha!"

He raised his glass of Perrier and gestured a toast.

"When I use you in a book, it's often with sentences that you actually uttered." (Sasha continued.) "You had a certain style of speaking as a therapist, an American style. So all the French analysts became quite intrigued by it. They even write learned monographs about this character, Akeret. So now the analysts are analyzing my fictitious analysis!"

"And what do they say?"

"They say that you are much too interventionist," Sasha said. "French analysts never say a word. Zombies! I think I would have done myself in a long time ago if I'd been analyzed by a Frenchman.

"Freud pervades people's lives over here without their really knowing it. I always say that after all the dictators of the twentieth century have disappeared—Hitler, Stalin, Franco— there is one man who has conquered us all, and that is Freud. Nobody can think about himself without in some way falling into his pattern of thought. To some people in France, it's beginning to be unbearable, but it's a fact.

"When I married Maria, I decided to learn German. I started to read Freud in the original, and it was an incredible experience. Besides everything else, he was a fabulous stylist. I became a kind of Freudian scholar from the literary perspective. I taught a course on Freud the writer. And pretty soon that influenced my entire critical perspective. Before, I approached literature from a existential point of reference; now it was psychoanalytical. I wrote a psychoanalytic interpretation of Proust that caused quite a stir.

"But it is in my novels where you find the greatest Freudian influence. Whenever I am interviewed on TV, I quote a letter that Freud wrote to Fliess: 'Since I discovered the unconscious, I find myself much more interesting.' Yes, yes, that is exactly what happened to me. I was not an introvert at all until we started our little psychic tug-of-war. All of a sudden there was a whole world to discover within. It was not an intellectual decision. People ask me, 'Why do you write about yourself?' They will ask me that again this afternoon at five o'clock when I am interviewed on television. And I will say, 'Why should I write about imaginary characters when everyone, if he goes deep enough within himself and exposes himself totally, is a novel?' I have even given this process a name, a name that sticks in France: autofiction."

Sasha suddenly stopped speaking and gazed at me. "Okay, Robert. I remember that skeptical look of yours. What are you thinking? Spit it out!"

"It's just that that only answers the question of why you write about yourself, but not the question of why you write at all," I said.

Sasha flashed me a mischievous smile.

"It's a good thing you *don't* speak French, Robert. They'd have you interviewing writers on television and making them squirm. I once said that I write in order to die less, but I don't say that anymore because a critic really gave it to me. He said that if I thought I was immortalizing myself in words, I was sadly mistaken. Maybe he's right. But so what? Who cares what happens after you are dead? What does it matter?"

An echo of that ancient look of despair flashed across Sasha's face. *What does it matter indeed?*

"I could use a little walk," I said after a moment. "How about you?"

"Fine, but we must go slowly and not too far. And first you must wait while I pee," he said.

I gazed after Sasha as he walked slowly inside the café to the WC. He looked so frail, so harmless. It was hard to think of him as a monster, no matter what ridiculous hateful things he said about women.

We walked a short way, then sat on a bench in a small park and watched a parade of well-turned-out Parisians stroll by. And then Sasha began to tell me about Maria, the young Austrian woman whom he had married and who had died five years ago.

When he was fifty-seven, Sasha had placed an advertisement for a female companion in a high-tone literary magazine. He had stated that he was a well-known writer, financially secure, looking for a European woman, twenty-five to forty, interested in literature and travel. Sixty-eight women had replied, and Sasha began interviewing them one at a time, starting with the youngest.

"There must have been a good dozen analysts who replied," Sasha said. "It is appalling how many lonely women analysts there are in Paris."

Maria, a twenty-six-year-old medical intern, intrigued Sasha from the start. She was beautiful and well read in three languages, but most important was what she had said to him at the end of their first meeting.

"She leaned over the [café] table and said, 'I am going to shock you,' and I said, 'I am hard to shock,' and she said, 'I love your smell. I need you to make love to me right now.' "

Sasha's eyes filled with tears as he told me this.

"Do you understand what an extraordinary moment that was, Robert? It has always been I who would say such a thing, make such a move. I was overwhelmed."

"Maybe you didn't really believe you were desirable anymore," I said.

"*Anymore?*" Sasha repeated with a melancholy laugh.

The affair with Maria began that night. It was passionately sexual, and just as in the old days, Sasha described it to me in exquisite detail. Maria moved in with him that week. They made love every day. They married three months later, and by the end of the year she was pregnant.

Here Sasha stopped and swallowed hard. He was obviously having difficulty continuing with the story.

"I don't know why this should be so hard," he said, finally. "God knows, it's public knowledge—at least wherever my books are read."

He took several deep breaths and then went on.

"We had an understanding: no children. That part of my life was over, and anyway, I'd made a mess of it. When we married, Maria had agreed wholeheartedly. It was even her idea to begin with, I think. She had her studies, her career, no room for children. But suddenly the hormones took possession of her, and she wanted to keep it. I told her that the choice was very clear, either me or the unborn child, so she relented and got an abortion.

"She had it done in a private clinic that was finally closed down by the medical authorities. They made a terrible job of it. After that we went to Switzerland for a rest, and she started to have horrible pains. The doctor gave her some pills which didn't help. Then she discovered that drinking was the only way to stop the pain."

"And she kept drinking?"

"Yes," Sasha said. "She kept drinking. And she also kept trying to get pregnant. Which she did, again and again, but now she couldn't hold onto the pregnancy, they'd botched her up so badly. The drinking got worse. She drank a liter of vodka a night. She had to stop working, of course. And after a while the situation was intolerable.

"I did the only thing I am able to do when my life starts to fall apart: I started a new book. It was, of course, about us—Maria and me. I gave her each chapter as I wrote it, and sometimes we'd talk about it. It was a very interesting process from a literary point of view—a character commenting on herself. She was a very acute critic, Maria.

"There is one chapter in which she is totally drunk for an entire day. It goes on and on, chronicling every clumsy gesture, every trip and fall, every incoherent utterance. It is not a pretty picture, but it is an accurate one. I gave it to Maria like all of the others, and then I left for a conference in Hamburg.

"I called our apartment as soon as I got to my hotel, but there was no answer. None the next day either, so I called the police. They knocked on our door—no answer. They broke in and found her on the floor. She had already been dead for a day."

Sasha gazed into the distance.

"That became part of my novel, of course. There are things that cannot be said. Usually they are said to an analyst in the closeness of professional secrecy. But I—I put them on the page. And when the book came out—that was in '89—that was all anyone talked about. Maria's death. Her suicide."

"Was it definitely a suicide?" I asked.

"No one knows." Sasha shrugged. "Her blood was full of alcohol, enough to kill her. But what her intention was, only she knows. I said that it was a suicide in the novel, though."

"Why?"

Sasha shrugged again.

"Because it felt right," he said. "Because a suicide corresponded to the guilt I felt. It made better literary sense."

*Better literary sense?* At that moment, all the revulsion that I had been holding back—forever *professionally* holding back—rose up inside me. I tried my best to hide it, but I am sure that Sasha could see it on my face. He said nothing about it, though.

"The book became quite *une cause.*" Sasha went on. "On one of the major talk shows the moderator accused me of murdering Maria by showing her that chapter."

"How did you respond to that?"

"I said, 'Yes, it is true, it was hard on her, but it was even harder on me.' There was a public commotion the next day. Letters in the papers, that sort of thing. People were scandalized. All of that was good for the book, of course. It became a best seller. And here is something interesting for you: As the book soared up in reputation and sales, I became more and more depressed. I was making a great deal of money and seeing beautiful women, but my body went dead. And then, finally, my penis died on me, too."

"You were seeing a new woman?"

"Yes, I started in with a Belgian woman just five months after burying Maria. People didn't like that. If you say that about a character in a book, it's fine, but here was a writer who said that about himself. On prime-time television I said the most terrible thing: I said, 'I have not ceased to love my wife, but if you don't kill the dead, they will kill you.'

"And it was around then that I couldn't do it anymore, when I started getting the injections. This is one area where French medicine is way ahead of the Americans. It is because impotency is a problem that causes the French much more anguish than it does Americans. The injection is not painful, but still, the woman hates it because she wants it to come naturally. Yet that is one thing science cannot do: It cannot create desire. No, no, not desire . . ." Sasha's voice trailed off, and he became silent.

I looked at my watch. It was past four o'clock. I knew that Sasha had to leave soon for his television interview.

"What are your plans now?" I asked.

Sasha gave me a pained smile.

"I know one thing for certain," he said. "I am a man of the twentieth century. I don't want to live one minute in the twenty-first. That is not my century.

"In the press, people ask, 'What will Alexandrovich write for a postscript? He has written five novels about himself; will there be another?' Yes, there will be one more book, though I will never see it published. When a man drowns, they say he sees his whole life in his head. I would like to rewrite what I wrote in the other books but without punctuation so that my whole life flashes by in an instant. I will call it *Diary of a Suicide*, and it will do something which no autobiographer has ever done: describe my own death. It would go right up to the moment when I swallow the death pills. My publisher will be thrilled. It would get so much publicity. It would have quite an impact."

"I'm sure it would," I said. "You'd be remembered."

Sasha looked deeply into my eyes. "That is why I write, Robert," he said.

"I hope there will be a few other books before that one," I said.

Sasha laughed.

WE TALKED a few minutes longer, and then Sasha had to leave. We had made tentative plans to see each other again the next day, but Sasha told me that he had a busy day, and I did not press him. I walked back with him to St.-Germain. We were almost at the metro stop when an attractive young woman suddenly popped up from a café seat and approached Sasha. She touched his arm and began speaking rapidly to him in French. I did not catch much of it, just enough to realize that she was one of his readers, a devotee, and that she greatly admired his honesty. As she spoke, the writer's face transformed from that of a desperate old man to that of a young lover.

# Epilogue: Final Analysis

Presume not that I am the thing I was.

William Shakespeare, *Henry IV, Part II*

I HAVE BEEN SITTING in my office for over a week now, waiting to come to rest. My traveling couch continues to swoop back and forth in time and place as I try to make sense of my journey. I feel exalted, humbled, inspired, confused.

In my absence the mail has piled up on my desk. One colleague sent me a *New Yorker* cartoon which shows a patient on a couch saying to her therapist, "Well, I do have this recurring dream that one day I might see some results."

Ah, yes, results. This trip was not simply the self-indulgence of a sexagenarian with an extravagant appetite for story endings; it was a pilgrimage for answers: Did I actually provide lasting help for my patients? Did they find the lives they were seeking? Was life sweeter, fuller than it would have been if we had never encountered one another?

Crucial questions. Impossible questions.

Also in my pile of correspondence is an article by Frederick Crews that a friend clipped from the *New York Review of Books*. It starts like this:

That psychoanalysis, as a mode of treatment, has been experiencing a long institutional decline is no longer in serious dispute. Nor is the reason: though some patients claim to have acquired profound

insight and even alterations of personality, in the aggregate psychoanalysis has proved to be an indifferently successful and vastly inef-
ficient method of removing neurotic symptoms. It is also the method
that is least likely to be "over when it is over." The experience of
undergoing intensive analysis may have genuine value as a form of
extended meditation, but it seems to provide many more converts
than cures.

Beneath the article I find a substantial packet of heated
replies and counterreplies that the article engendered in the
pages of that magazine for months thereafter: psychotherapists angrily defending their turf; Professor Crews attacking
them as pseudo-scientists without a clue to the protocols of
the scientific method. Strangely none of this touches me. I
have no illusions that this enterprise of mine was a scientific
experiment.

The truth is, none of the scientific methods for judging the
results of therapy mean much to me either, though for a very
simple and quite possibly naïve reason: because I do not believe individual lives are comparable. I do not believe that any
experiment that compares the results of Person A, who has
been in therapy, with Person B, who has not been in therapy,
with Person C, who has been in "placebo" therapy, can yield
data that will be meaningful to me. This is because no matter
how similar Persons A, B, and C may be in terms of their presenting problems and personalities, I shall always be struck
by their differences—the differences that make each of them
unique, the differences that will stay with them throughout
their lives.

To whom would I compare Naomi? To another woman
who copes with pathologically low self-esteem by adopting
an alternative identity? Would any alternative identity do, or
would it have to be as a flamenco dancer? And if so, would it
have to be as a flamenco dancer who is escaping from an abusive childhood at the hands of a self-loathing mother? Would
anything less than these similarities miss what is absolutely

essential about Naomi? Would anything less be able to account for her unique abilities to cope and change? And who would be my "control" for Charles? Would simply another zoophilic do, or would it have to be another man who lusts after a polar bear? Who for Seth? Who for Sasha?

For better or for worse, I have always thought of psychotherapy more as an art than a science and of myself as more of a lyrical therapist than a doctrinaire theoretician. So I am inclined to evaluate the results of my work in the same ways I would evaluate other artwork: subjectively, intuitively, aesthetically—with imagination and leaps of faith. But even within this slippery context, I still want to know the same thing that the scientist does: whether or not therapy did help my patients to lead "better" lives—*whatever that means.*

One thing it can mean is that a patient reports that he *feels* better after therapy and that he continued to feel that way generally in the years that followed. That, for example, Naomi was freed from her feelings of self-hate for the rest of her life; that Seth was able to leave his stultifying depressions behind him; that Mary was no longer overcome by feelings of rage and guilt.

None of these three patients was able to report a "perfect cure" to me in this sense. Naomi had a relapse wherein she suffered her mother's abuse for eight more years, during which those awful feelings of self-hatred returned to torture her. And Seth, after decades of feeling increasingly stronger, happier, and more positive, was suddenly overcome by a terrible depression—what he called a "divine blight"—which only the passage of time was able to heal. Of these three patients, only Mary was able to say that the feelings that had brought her into my office in the first place—the rage at being treated as an inferior in her family, the guilt over "willing" her father's death—had left her for good after therapy. Yet even Mary admitted that deep in her heart she would forever long for a loving father. She did not believe that therapy could ever quell *that* feeling of emptiness. No, none of them lived completely happily ever after.

But the operative word is *generally*—and these three patients reported *generally* feeling much better in their lives following therapy than they had in the years leading up to therapy. No, there are no controls with which to compare these resulting feelings; I cannot say for sure that any or all of these three individuals would not have felt better simply with the passage of time, with what used to be called quite reasonably "growing out" of a bad patch of life. I can only go by the gut response that these patients and I shared: that therapy was somehow responsible for their generally feeling so much better.

Yet I certainly cannot say that of the other two patients I visited; neither Charles nor Sasha felt significantly better when I saw them these many years later than they had felt when I first encountered them. Sasha now suffered from feelings of extreme loneliness and despair; he took antidepressants to get through the day; he was toying with suicide, albeit as much for literary reasons as to escape his depression. And Charles, too, felt lonely and somewhat benumbed. "Crazy" as Charles had been when I first saw him, he was more passionate then than now, more passionately in love and hence, I believe, more passionately alive. The same could be said about Sasha in the midst of his extramarital affairs—passionate, full of feelings. Of course, both were in a more passionate stage of life then. But to be fair, there is the distinct possibility that it was therapy itself that at least robbed Charles of his strongest and deepest feelings, robbed him of feelings in the name of personal survival.

Sasha would be the first to differentiate between "feeling good" and "passionately feeling." For him, "feeling good" is banal, insignificant stuff compared with the feelings of the passionately lived life. From his existential point of view, it is better to be passionately miserable than to be mindlessly blissful. Many psychotherapists passionately agree with Sasha; to them, simply "feeling good" smacks of Brave New Worldism, especially in this age when "mood brighteners" like Prozac and Zoloft are being substituted for depth therapy. One of the side benefits of Prozac is that it has forced those of us who practice "talk" therapy to define more closely what it is that we are trying to do if it is not just to make our patients feel better.

When Fromm posited biophilia as the goal of therapy, he was not talking about simply feeling good. Biophilia represents feeling *fully alive,* being more able to participate in a full range of emotions (including grief, compassion, and sorrow as well as exaltation, passion, and joy) and being able to live productively. It suggests an awareness of life's possibilities and an attitude of hope and love toward all of life. Biophilia's opposite, necrophilia, represents an attitude of despair and negation, a withdrawal from life, and a mode of being that defeats life's possibilities.

By this standard, of the five patients I visited, Seth probably traveled the farthest from necrophilia toward biophilia in the course of therapy and thereafter. (I suppose it is no coincidence that Seth is the one patient of this group whom I worked with under Fromm's guidance.) When I first encountered Seth, he fantasized about himself as a mechanical object; when I saw him decades later in New Mexico, he was surely one of the most centered, life-embracing people I have ever met. At one point during our long Albuquerque night together, I asked Seth if he thought there were any experiences in his life that he believes would have been denied him if he had not undergone therapy, and he answered, "*All* of my experiences after therapy were made possible by it." Even Seth's staggering midlife descent into depression, deathly as it was, ultimately was experienced by him as a response to becoming more fully alive at a time when he was not yet ready for it—

"opening the windows" too quickly. I can imagine Seth's response to Professor Crews's dismissal of analysis as merely "a form of extended meditation": *"My God, what could be more enriching than an extended meditation?"*

On Fromm's necrophilia-biophilia scale, Mary seems an indisputable winner, too. She entered therapy in a deep depression that was only relieved by bursts of anger and other "acting out," and she left therapy feeling strong and loving, happily committed to both her work and her family of creation. When I visited Mary in Northern California, I found a woman not only filled with love for life but dedicated to passing that love along, taking her place in what she viewed as the "chain reaction" of loving care. She had clearly attained Fromm's therapeutic goal of a "loving attitude" toward life. This should not be construed as some saccharine greeting card ideal; rather, it is the logical conclusion of the existential syllogism that to live fully, one must love life.

Naomi fared well by Fromm's criteria, too. She arrived in my City College cubicle feeling alienated and dead, and she left feeling vibrant and confident—albeit vibrant and confident *as someone else!* In the years that followed, she had briefly fallen back under the spell of her necrophilic mother, and even when I visited her in Florida, she was still unable to embrace completely her native identity as a Jew. But from what I experienced of her that day, Naomi was living life to the fullest, not retreating from it. What could be better testament to biophilia than when she joyfully declared to me, "Isn't it wonderful . . . the way you can be so many people in one lifetime?"

I am sure there are many therapists who would call that statement "insane," the ravings of a woman with multiple personality disorder. Not me. I call it a declaration of love of life. And I'd like to think that Fromm would call it that, too.

One particularly elusive criterion for how well a course of therapy has worked is whether or not it affected a "core change" in the patient's personality. Fromm was alluding to this when he compared "re-forming" a patient's behavior with repairing a slum: "If you make a few repairs here and there in a slum, it's still a slum."

Sometimes I can put my finger on this distinction; sometimes I cannot. What constitutes the continuous "core" self has bedeviled philosophers and psychologists since the Greeks. I do know that when Sasha wanted me just to do a little "tinkering," that felt wrong; I believed that we would have to go deeper than that to effect any meaningful change in his life. And one thing I can say without a shred of doubt is that Naomi had an indisputable core change: She changed identities. Or is that too much of a change?

In a book I read on the plane back from Paris, I came across a reference to a case of Milton Erickson's in which an energetic young patient insisted that he was Jesus Christ; Erickson's treatment was to find the young man a job as a carpenter. Perhaps Erickson was practicing the ultimate in Christ-inspired therapy: He was not judging his patient, just facilitating his self-realization. But he was not giving him any personal insight.

One thing that psychotherapy can do that Prozac can never do is provide a patient with knowledge of himself. Fromm wrote that psychoanalysis should be seen "not as a therapy, but as an instrument for self understanding . . . an instrument in the art of living. . . ."

This knowledge would include the salient themes of one's life, an identification of one's true desires and the conflicts that surround them, the differences between difficulties created by external reality and those created by internal fantasy.

But self-knowledge in itself is no guarantee that a person will feel better or even change destructive patterns of behavior. All we have to do is think of Sasha to realize that, although, of course, Sasha believed that therapy had done him a world of good.

For me, this goes to the nitty-gritty of the question of what it means for a patient to get better. Whose notion of "better"—mine or the patient's? The therapist Carl Rogers warned that "it is a dangerous philosophy to assume the right to be the self-appointed authority on what is best for someone else." And Dr. Szasz put it even more bluntly, "Therapy is like religion: there should be a free choice."

But if I allow my patients to pick their own therapeutic goal, when can I feel confident that they are ready to make this choice? In the depths of depression? At the height of mania?

My personal answer is another murky one: Patients are ready to make this decision at the point when they know themselves well enough to understand that decision's implications. But after that Szasz is right: Free choice must reign.

In thirty-five years of practicing psychotherapy, no one has tested me more formidably on this issue than Sasha Alexandrovich. Even now, after visiting him in Paris, I remain conflicted. Above all, Sasha's goal in therapy was to get back to creating art. He succeeded in this fabulously, and he makes a convincing case that he owes it all to his therapy with me; the subject of his art is himself; therapy revealed himself to himself in a way that he was able to transform into art. Thus, by his own lights, therapy was wonderfully successful. But this makes me think of Crews's assertion that therapy has won "more converts than cures." Sasha was converted to the psychoanalytic framework for understanding himself and others, yet his life seems untouched by this understanding. And Sasha's life pains me deeply. It seems necrophilic in the extreme: He treats himself as an object with his pills and injections; he cannot truly love another human being; he loves life so little that he would sacrifice it for the sake of a good book. By Fromm's standards, therapy has failed miserably with Sasha.

Or has it? If, for Sasha, creating transcendent art is the ultimate in being aware and alive, who am I to say that he is necrophilic? Shouldn't I rather say that his necrophilic life feeds his biophilic art and that art is the life he has chosen?

But I will never be completely comfortable with that idea. God help me, if Sasha does write *Diary of a Suicide,* I know I will feel that I failed him.

It is just the opposite that pains me about Charles. I am quite sure that I helped him save his biological life; without that, of course, he would have had nothing. But I was unable to help him find a very satisfying life to replace the passionate (albeit suicidal) one that I turned him away from. I did not have enough time for more than crisis intervention with Charles. I wish I could have given him more. But honestly, I am not sure how much more I could have given him.

And that brings me to my ultimate question: How can I know if I am responsible for whatever gains my patients made in their lives? That is to say, even if I were absolutely clear on what "getting better" meant, how could I be sure that therapy was the cause and not something else?

Seth provides an interesting case in point. Between the last time I saw him in 1968 and when I visited him twenty-six years later, he had immersed himself in a good two dozen varieties of therapy and spiritual growth programs, ranging from Rolfing to vision quests. What, if anything, in his therapy with me can be credited for the tremendous changes he made in his life?

I asked him that question at one point in my visit. Seth laughed and said, "They *all* deserve credit, and so does every person I have met, for that matter. I am the sum of all my experiences. But my therapy with you set me on this path, and for that I am eternally grateful."

I want very much to believe him, of course.

Citing a study of therapy outcomes done by Lester Luborsky, Professor Crews raises the question of how much we can credit the particular content of therapy with whatever "cure" follows it. Crews says, "No doubt it is motivationally useful for each of the myriad extant psychotherapies to offer its clients some structure of belief—whether it be about undoing infantile repression, contacting the inner child, surrendering to the collective unconscious, or reliving previous incarnations—but as Luborsky understood, such notions are window dressing for the more mundane and mildly effective process of renting a solicitous helper."

I should rage against this kind of attack, I know, but I do not. Maybe I am getting old and running low on passionate anger. But I like to think that my love for my patients is finally maturing to the point where it does not really matter to me who or what takes the credit for their cure. I am just so very grateful and happy to see them living satisfying lives no matter what the reason.

Truth to tell, I would not really mind if Professor Crews proved that the therapy I gave my patients turned out to be nothing more than some handholding and a sympathetic ear, the simple work of a "solicitous helper." Actually I would take great pride in that. I think I do it well.

As I look back over my follow-up journey, something Seth said comes to mind. "You're greedy to find out if what you dedicated your whole life to has amounted to anything."

Well, I do feel I made a difference. I sometimes wonder if in the coming century psychotherapy will be viewed as some kind of arcane witchcraft, a clumsy and attenuated method of transformation and self-knowledge that my grandchildren will think of in the same way that I now think of exorcisms. Yet not even this thought upsets me. I keep thinking of the time when Mary's son, Jared, asked me, "So, what's the verdict? Does therapy work?" And Mal answered for me, "Maybe it only works when it works."

That, in the end, is all I could have asked for.

THE COUCH FINALLY SETTLES in my office. I find myself remembering something Fromm once said to me: "I see each patient as the hero of an epic poem."

I have always liked that idea, but I don't believe I fully

understood it until I took my journey. Until now I did not appreciate the sheer epic proportions of a person's life. The mere fact that in spite of all the obstacles they faced, Naomi and Charles and Seth and Mary and Sasha could make their ways from youth into middle age touches me deeply. I have returned from my travels awed by the capacity of Man to survive; that, in itself, strikes me as heroic. And nothing that therapy can or cannot do compares with it.

*Drawing by Paul Bacon*

# Acknowledgments

I F, AS I HOPE, this book reads like a novel, it is because my notes, recorded interviews, recollections and analysis were rendered into a narrative by my friend and colleague Daniel Martin Klein, a novelist. This book literally could not have been written without him.

Above all, I want to express my deepest appreciation to my patients who so graciously welcomed me back into their lives and made possible this remarkable journey.

I am forever indebted to Rollo May, my teacher, colleague, and friend. He will be sorely missed.

I wish to thank Howard Morhaim, my literary agent, who never faltered in his belief in the value of this book, and Susan Barrows Munro, my editor at W. W. Norton, who envisioned from the start what this book could be and then cheered me on.

For his good advice as well as the use of his library, I want to thank Dr. David Lippman. For their close readings of the manuscript in progress, I thank Daniel's wife, Freke Vuijst, and Dr. Peter Roemer. For their clear-minded opinions about specific passages, I thank my good friend, Donna Jackson, and my daughter, Kim Cookson.

My appreciation also goes to John Daniel for his patient and careful transcription of the follow-up tapes.

Finally, to *min aller beste venn* and loving wife, Ann, who continues to be a wise and caring anchor through all my twists and turns while practicing this fabulous profession of psychoanalysis.